Herbs

HOW TO GROW AND USE THEM

BY JACQUELINE HÉRITEAU

GROSSET
GOOD LIFE
BOOKS

PUBLISHERS • GROSSET & DUNLAP • NEW YORK

Acknowledgments

Cover photograph by Mort Engel
Drawings by Peter Kalberkamp

To Adelma Simmons, the *grande dame* of herb knowledge, my thanks for the photographic sequence on making tussie-mussies; to Kate Alfriend, Office of Communications, U.S. Department of Agriculture, and to Elvin McDonald, senior editor, *House Beautiful* magazine, my thanks for help with photographs and specialized information on growing herbs around the country; to Peter Kalberkamp for the herb garden planting plans and drawings; to Francesca Bosetti Morris, for superb Italian recipes using basil and tarragon; to the American Spice Trade Association for the *Dictionary of Herbs* illustrations; and to editor Lee Schryver, for wanting to see this book made as varied as possible, my very sincere gratitude.

I am most indebted to all the Hériteau clan in France—aunts, uncles, and cousins—and to my father, Marcel Hériteau, who taught me how to grow and use the herbs.

My thanks to the following for their permission to use the illustrations in this book: American Spice Trade Institute: p. 55 right, p. 61, p. 71, p. 74 top, p. 74 bottom, p. 85; Ralph Bailey: p. 11 left; Hort-Pix: p. 9, p. 10 bottom left, p. 10 right, p. 11 top right, p. 16 left, p. 17 left, p. 18 top left, p. 18 bottom left, p. 18 right, p. 19 bottom left, p. 19 top right, p. 21 top left, p. 21 bottom left, p. 23 left; Frank Lusk: p. 35 bottom, p. 36 top left, p. 36 bottom left, p. 36 right, p. 47 top left, p. 47 top right, p. 47 bottom left, p. 47 bottom right; Elvin McDonald: p. 6 top left, p. 6 bottom left, p. 6 right, p. 7, p. 11 bottom right, p. 16 bottom, p. 19 top left, p. 19 bottom right, p. 20, p. 23 top right, p. 23 bottom right, p. 24 top left, p. 24 bottom left, p. 24 top right, p. 24 bottom right, p. 25 top left, p. 25 bottom left, p. 25 top right, p. 25 bottom right, p. 26 top left, p. 26 bottom left, p. 26 right, p. 29 bottom, p. 30 top left, p. 30 top right, p. 30 bottom left, p. 30 bottom right, p. 31 left, p. 31 right, p. 41; The New York Botanical Garden: p. 16 top; New York Public Library: p. 35 top, p. 39 top, p. 49 left, p. 49 right, p. 50, p. 51, p. 52, p. 53, p. 54, p. 55 left, p. 57, p. 58, p. 59, p. 60, p. 63, p. 64, p. 66, p. 67, p. 68, p. 70 right, p. 72, p. 75, p. 77, p. 78, p. 79, p. 80, p. 83, p. 84 left, p. 84 right, p. 87, p. 88, p. 89; United States Department of Agriculture: p. 22 top left, p. 22 bottom left, p. 22 right.

Contents

A. All thefe fquare muſt be ſet with Trees, the Garden and other Ornaments muſt ſtand in ſpaces, betwixt the Trees, and in the borders and fences.

B. Trees twenty yards aſunder.

C. Garden Knots.

D. Kitching Garden.

E. Bridge.

F. Conduit.

G. Stairs.

H. Walks ſet with great wood thick.

I. Walks ſet with great wood round about your Orchard.

K. The Out fence.

L. The Out fence ſet with ſtone-fruit.

M. Mount. To force Earth for a Mount or ſuch like, ſet it round with quick, and lay boughs of Trees ſtrangely intermingled, the tops inward, with the Earth in the middle.

N. Still houſe.

O. Good ſtanding for Bees, if you have an houſe.

P. If the River run by your door, and under your Mount, it will be pleaſant.

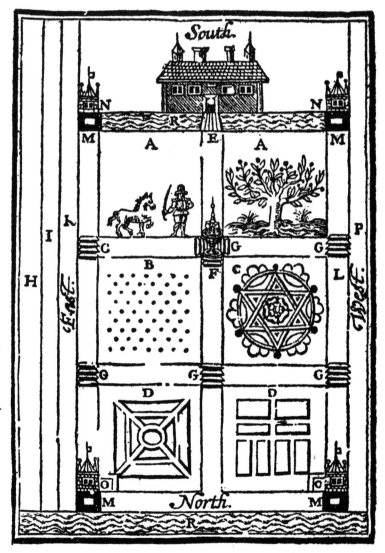

PART I
Seasoning, Scents, and Gardens

1 The Magical Herbs

Plant Your Own *Bouquet Garni,* Pick Your Own Moth Repellent, Grow Your Own Herbal Shampoo

Long before freeze-dried chives and aerosol perfumes, fields and woods and herb gardens supplied the homemaker with everything needed to flavor foods, and to perfume the homes we lived in, our closets, our linens and woolens.

Cooking with herbs and using the herbs to make potpourris and bath bags, fragrant vinegars, rubbing lotions, and the little nosegays called tussie-mussies are adventures the good gardener can pursue for very little investment in time and money. A few make excellent ground covers, both scented and flowering. Herbs are undemanding and versatile plants, humble in their needs, generous in their gifts. The basil that makes *Pasta al Pesto* a culinary miracle grows easily almost anywhere, including on a sunny windowsill, and doubles as a fragrant leaf to use in dry perfumes. The thyme you use to cover any barren spot in the garden, anchor the drifting soil of a slope, trim and train into a handsome terrace plant, is flavor for a host of foods and scent in dozens of aromatic herb mixtures for perfuming clothing.

Whether you live in an apartment, a suburban house, or right out in the open country, growing herbs for flavoring and for fragrance is one of the happiest and most interesting of all ways to indulge your gardening instincts.

Almost everybody has been tempted into buying a pot of parsley or a clump of chives when spring is on us and the supermarkets are selling aromatic greens for growing. But we really haven't got all we can from herbs until we know names like chervil and sorrel and basil and bay. We haven't really cooked with herbs until we've learned to use coriander and cumin, fennel and ginger root, and have made candied violets and our own caraway vinegar. Even then, we're only beginners.

There's a whole world of fragrant herbs our grandmothers knew. Remember that faint, subtle, hard-to-define fragrance that came from linens and closets, bureau drawers, and creaky old trunks in the attic? Those

Chervil (Anthriscus cerefolium)

Basil (Ocimum basilicum)

Parsley *(Petroselinum crispum)*

scents weren't accidents of old wood in old houses. They were deliberate. They were grown and dried, crushed and combined, sewn into little sachets and muslin bags, tied up in fragrant tussie-mussies, and tucked away here and there and everywhere. Our grandmothers knew how to make a house

and everything in it smell faintly, faintly, like ... we were never sure what. Was it southernwood? Was it wormwood? Dried roses? Lavender cotton? Lemon balm? Moneywort? Each and all were mixed in combinations inherited from the family memory chest, devised and improvised from the silvery gray-greens growing in the herb garden.

Gardens of the distant past provided herbs for the spice shelf for extra-special eating, the perfumery for extraordinary fragrance, and medicinal herbs for the pharmacy. Cleopatra strewed rose petals to capture Mark Antony's fancy. The Greeks crowned guests with parsley to improve their appetites and serenity. To the Greeks, thyme was a masculine perfume, a symbol of elegance; to the Elizabethans, it was an ingredient in a concoction that could enable one to see the fairies. Rosemary was a symbol for lovers (remember Ophelia's heartsick lines to Hamlet?) and a sprig of the herb was still sent on St. Valentine's Day in colonial America. Rue, southernwood, sweet woodruff, tansy, and wormwood cleared the air in the sickroom and were prized remedies for all manner of ills from "worms in the ears" to baldness and poisoning.

It was in Elizabethan times that the herb garden became an elaborate affair, in keeping with the importance herbs played in making life pleasant and safe. In knot gardens, ropes of clipped lavender hedges and silvery sages twined symmetrically around each other, entwining contrasting shades and textures of aromatic foliage. The formal herb garden could cover acres and take years to bring to perfection. In colonial Williamsburg, centuries later, reflections of these giant herbal enterprises appeared in miniature, and everywhere in America that people went, culinary, medicinal, and fragrance herbs grew.

Today the formal herb garden is rare, but in every landscape, if only in the "landscape" of the indoor garden, there is room for at least a few of these charming and very useful plants for seasoning.

Thyme *(Thymus argenteus)*

2
Herbs or Spices?

For years I've tried to get a clear picture on the difference between an herb and a spice. I've never read two books that agreed 100 percent on which was which. But as a sweeping generalization (that won't stand up to all arguments) spices seem to be dried, fragrant bits of bark and seeds which come from the Far East and tropical regions, while herbs seem to be (and this is not a correct horticultural definition) green, herbaceous, as opposed to woody, plants whose leaves or flowers, and sometimes seeds as well, are used for flavoring and fragrance, either fresh or dried. For instance, green peppers and chili peppers seem to be called herbs, while black and white peppercorns are apparently classed as spices.

The American Spice Trade Association in Englewood Cliffs, New Jersey, says the spice trade goes back before recorded history. Archaeologists estimate that by 50,000 B.C. primitives were using aromatic plants (spices or herbs?) to make food taste better. And from hieroglyphics on the walls of Egyptian pyramids and from the Bible, we know herbs and spices played vital roles in the lives and finances of the times. Caravans along the trade routes of antiquity with as many as 4,000 camels carried spices and merchandise from the East, from the Orient, Calicut, and Goa to the markets in Nineveh and Babylon. The road from Gilead to Egypt was part of the "golden road to Samarkand," along which traveled peppers and cloves from India, cinnamon and nutmeg from the Spice Islands, and ginger from China. Ginger is covered in this book, but I can't say whether it's an herb or a spice. Many spice writers seem to include herbs among spices (clearly going too far) along with plants like celery and onion that can hardly be classed as either.

Spices in the ancient world were so extraordinarily expensive that only the wealthy could afford them. Some were even used as money—pepper notably.

The importance of spices in early times is easier to understand when we remember that there was no refrigeration and that foods spoiled quickly. A few spices helped to preserve them, and many certainly went a long way toward disguising unfortunate food flavors. They still do: To improve a tasteless supermarket chicken, rub 1 teaspoon of a good curry over it before baking, and to enrich the flavor of a not-so-good beef roast, before roasting, encase it in a coat of prepared mustard mixed with 2 peeled and crushed cloves of garlic.

Since herbs and spices also helped to disguise unfortunate odors, they came to be used—alone or together—to make fragrant burned, boiled, and dried perfumes. In fact, here were the forerunners of our entire perfume industry.

3
What to Grow?
A List of Favorite Herbs

Below is a list of the herbs covered in this book. The list includes 42 herbs—30 of the best flavoring or culinary herbs, some 20 herbs for fragrance (some culinary herbs are fragrance herbs), and a few herbs with special uses—catnip for cat lovers, violets to candy, chamomile to make hair rinses and shampoos, and ground covers.

Silvery sage, thyme, and rosemary grow comfortably at the foot of a spear-leafed yucca in a small garden surrounded by cement stepping-stones and bordered by a patio. Their silvery green foliage is fragrant at noon and blends well with the surroundings, taking little or no care.

Chamomile (Roman) (Anthemis nobilis)

Many of the 30 culinary herbs are also used to make potpourris, sachets, sweet bags for linens and moth repellents. A few that are not noted as fragrance herbs are nonetheless included in some recipes for fragrance — anise seed, for instance. And some herbs used mainly to make fragrances are occasionally used in cooking, such as lemon balm, which makes a delightful tea.

If you have lots of space, you can grow all the herbs. One or two plants of each is usually enough, unless you are going into the herb business. You can grow a dozen herbs in just a few square feet of garden space. Use a few in a flowering border, some in a foundation planting group, the most useful culinary herbs by the kitchen door, the fragrance herbs, tall and small, anywhere near the main entrance or terrace, wherever there is sun and well-drained soil. My choices, if I could grow only 20, or only 10, or only 5, appear below. If I could grow only 1 herb, it would be parsley.

Woolly thyme with a variegated leaf spills gracefully over a rock outcropping. Like many other prostrate forms of the popular herbs, woolly thyme can be used to soften almost any problem area in the home garden.

Rosemary in bloom (right) backed by lavender cotton's feathery pale spires helps turn a rocky mound into an attractive setting for a modern house.

With no gardening space at all, grow your herbs in containers on terrace or patio, or apartment roof, in a sunny window, on a small balcony, or under lights in a closet or the hallway. The perennial herbs make good houseplants since most come from hot, dry areas where the climate isn't all that different from the hot, dry indoors of centrally-heated homes. A few herbs need chilling in winter. The "Dictionary of Culinary and Fragrant Herbs," Part IV, tells which herbs do, and what to do about it.

Some spices that cannot be admitted to the rank of herbals are cardamon, cinnamon, cloves, fenugreek, mustard, nutmeg, paprika, poppyseed, saffron, sesame seed, and turmeric. They are often found on the seasoning shelf along with herbs, of course, and some of them can be grown in your own garden.

In medieval times, many flowers were considered to be medicinal herbs, and today we use some of them as edible garnishes and in potpourris—iris, madonna lily, marigold,

Geraniums in various forms will grow up or down slopes, a quality that makes them suitable for a place in almost any landscape. The scented-leaved varieties belong in the herb garden and can be used as culinary herbs as well as for scenting potpourris.

Rosemary—here in the form called Rosmarinus officinalis, *which is upright—withstands extraordinarily poor growing conditions and brings fragrance as well as beauty to lots, corners, and difficult places.*

Sorrel *(Rumex acetosa)*

List of Favorite Herbs

	Other Uses	Height	Perennial	Annual	Culinary	Fragrance	My Choicest 20	10	5
Anise (*Pimpinella anisum*)		2'-3'		x	x	x			
Basil (*Ocimum basilicum*)		1'-2'		x	x	x	x	x	x
Bay Laurel (*Laurus nobilis*)		tree			x	x			
Borage (*Borago officinalis*)	dried bouquets	1½'-3'		x	x				
Caraway (*Carum carvi*)		2½'		biennial	x				
Catnip (*Nepeta cataria*)	for cats	3'-4'	x						
Chamomile (*Anthemis nobilis*)	ground cover, hair rinse	3"-12"	x						
Chervil (*Anthriscus cerefolium*)		6"-12"		x	x				
Chives (*Allium schoenoprasum*)	edible flowers	12"-15"	x		x		x	x	x
Coriander (*Coriandrum sativum*)		18"		x		x	x		
Costmary (*Chrysanthemum balsamita*)		5'-6'	x		x	x			
Cumin (*Cuminum cyminum*)		6"		x	x	x	x		
Dill (*Anethum graveolens*)		2'-3'		x	x		x	x	x
Fennel (*Foeniculum,* all species)		2'-4'	x	x	x		x		
Garlic (*Allium sativum*)		18"-24"		x	x				
Geranium (*Pelargonium,* all scented species)		2'-4'	x		x	x	x	x	
Ginger Root (*Zingiber officinale*)		18"-24"	x		x	x	x		
Lavender (*Lavandula,* all species)	hedge	3'-4'	x			x	x	x	x
Lavender Cotton (*Santolina chamaecyparissus*)	dried bouquets, hedge	1'-2'	x			x	x		
Lemon Balm (*Melissa officinalis*)		24"	x		x	x			
Lemon Verbena (*Lippia citriodorata*)		3'-10'	x		x	x			
Marjoram (*Majorana hortensis*)		8"-12"	x	x	x	x			
Mint (*Mentha,* all species)		18"-24"	x		x	x	x		
Moneywort (*Lysimachia nummularia*)	ground cover	1"-2"	x			x			
Nasturtium (*Tropaeolum,* all species)		12"-18"	x	x	x				
Oregano (*Origanum vulgare*)		24"-30"	x		x		x		
Parsley (*Petroselinum crispum*)		12"		biennial	x		x	x	x
Pennyroyal (*Mentha pulegium*)	ground cover	4"-6"	x						

List of Favorite Herbs

	Other Uses	Height	Perennial	Annual	Culinary	Fragrance	My Choicest 20	10	5
Peppers (*Capsicum annuum*)		18"-24"		x	x		x		
Rose (*Rosa*, all species)	edible flowers	3'-10'	x		x	x	x	x	
Rosemary (*Rosmarinus officinalis*)	ground cover, hedge	2'-6'	x		x	x			
Rue (*Ruta graveolens*)		2'-3'	x			x			
Sage (*Salvia*, all species)		2'-3'	x		x				
Savory (*Satureja*, all species)		12"-18"	x	x	x				
Shallots (*Allium ascalonicum*)		12"		x	x		x		
Sorrel (*Rumex*, all species)		2'-3'	x	x	x				
Southernwood (*Artemisia abrotanum*)		3'-5'	x			x	x	x	
Sweet Woodruff (*Asperula odorata*)	ground cover	8"	x		x	x	x	x	
Tansy (*Tanacetum vulgare*)		2'-3'	x			x			
Tarragon (*Artemisia dracunculus*)		20"	x		x	x	x	x	
Thyme (*Thymus*, all species)	ground cover	4"-10"	x		x	x	x		
Violet (*Viola*, all species)	edible flowers	8"-12"	x		x	x			
Wormwood (*Artemisia*, all species)	ground cover	2'-4'	x			x			

peony, primrose, columbine, and others. And many true herbs were purely medicinal. Most are no longer used today—clary, elecampane, hyssop, mallow, feverfew, poison hemlock, houseleek (hen-and-chickens), mandrake, opium poppy, pennyroyal, spurge, vervain, among others. The Chinese still use Gingseng root for virility in old age, as well as other herbs for cures. Today many are grown by herb specialists for purely historical reasons. They are mentioned here because you may encounter them in flowershops as ornamental plants.

Instructions for preparing the herbs—picking, drying, crushing, and grinding them—to make potpourris and tussie-mussies appear in Part III.

4
Where to Site the Herbs

If most of the spices come from the far East, most of the herbs we use today have come to us from Asia and the shores of the Mediterranean, and a few from South America. Most are perennial, many are evergreen in mild climates, and nearly all prefer hot sun and sandy, loose, well-drained—even poor—soil. Which is to say that herbs aren't hard to succeed with. If you have no soil, grow them in pots.

Kitchen Herbs

You can grow the culinary herbs in window boxes by the kitchen door, or by the doorstep in garden soil. Because the herbs tend to be straggly unless frequently clipped, an herb border should be planned even if its intent is totally casual. Grow the low ones in front, the tall ones behind. Or encase the herbs in symmetrical forms—in a cartwheel, in a ladder.

One of the handiest ways to handle the kitchen herbs is to build a pyramid contained in terraces formed by strips of corrugated metal.

A Formal Herb Garden

A formal garden for herbs demands an investment in time and space. The spot must be sunny, the soil loose and well drained, or it must be made so. The form is traditionally symmetrical: a square, a rectangle, a circle, a pair of half circles, a long, elegant oval, or two half ovals divided by a path.

After you have selected a site, mark out the bed with strings and stakes, and lay out areas in well-defined patterns—squares, circles, or regular free-form patches that repeat. On paper note which herb will go where. Plan a low hedge to outline the garden. Select plants that will offer contrast in foliage and texture, not quite as easy a job with herbs as with flowers, since the herbs belong to only a few basic family groups and resemble each other. Include herbs that will flower. A sea of gray-greens can be boring. Geraniums, in particular the scented-leaved geraniums used to perfume potpourris and in jellies and jams for flavoring, deserve a place in the herb border. Though roses, grown for their perfumed petals, aren't usually included in formal herb borders, nasturtiums with their edible flowers and spicy leaves can be. Chives bloom in pink, and there is a Chinese variety of white chives. A look at the "Dictionary of Culinary and Fragrant Herbs" (Part IV) will suggest which of your favorites can be counted on to bring color to the formal herb garden.

To make the formal herb garden easier to keep through the years, divide with sunken boards or corrugated metal or plastic, with an area for each herb or group of similar herbs. Many herbs spread by underground runners, and the dividers will help to keep them at home.

One of the important definitions of a formal herb garden is a path or system of paths leading through it. The paths help you to get at the plants for gardening chores, and invite walks through the garden when it is at its most fragrant—at noon, or after showers.

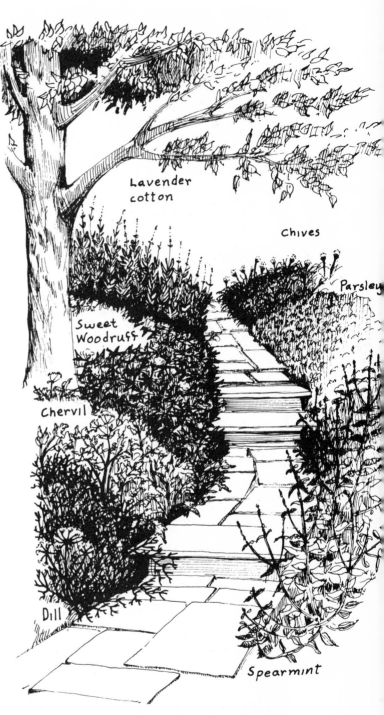

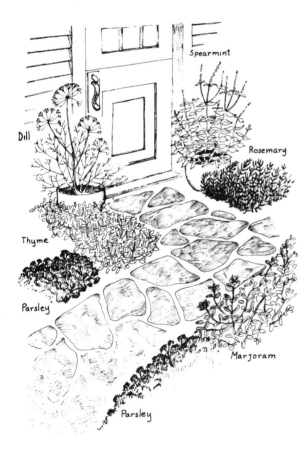

Kitchen herb garden grows where it is handiest to the cook—right by the kitchen door. It includes parsley, marjoram, thyme, rosemary, dill, and spearmint.

Casual approach to growing herbs places them along a garden path. Dill, chervil, spearmint, parsley, sweet woodruff, lavender cotton, and chives bloom, each in its season, and supply leaves for use fresh, and plenty for drying. High cut of tree branches allows enough sunlight for these herbs, which can stand more shade than many others.

Where to Site the Herbs 15

An example of a formal knot garden at the New York Botanical Garden, showing the careful shaping of herb plants for a decorative effect.

A big patch of parsley grows in a small formal bed with roses. Parsley is probably the most useful of all the culinary herbs and one of the easiest to locate because the bright green foliage fits in anywhere a low-growing green accent is suitable.

Chives (Allium schoenoprasum)

Grass, or a low-growing fragrant herb such as chamomile, is the traditional covering for an herb garden path. Go Elizabethan and build a mounded earth seat by the garden and grow chamomile over it.

To help in the planning of a formal herb garden, the list in chapter 3 indicates heights and characteristics—perennial, annual, evergreen—of the herbs. List your choices, and study the information given for each choice in the "Dictionary of Culinary and Fragrant Herbs" (Part IV). Mix and match, change and experiment on paper before you do any digging.

Herbs for Ground Cover

Thyme, chamomile, wormwood, moneywort, sweet woodruff, and prostrate rosemary are popular herbs often used as ground covers, and as lawn substitutes.

The herb used most often this way is probably Mother-of-Thyme. It's a low-growing, shrubby plant that makes a mat of tiny soft green leaves that give off a heavy scent when crushed. It's great on dry slopes and can be propagated by seed or cuttings rooted and planted 12 inches apart. It produces small lavender flowers. There are white, silver, and gold creeping thymes as well, some with red

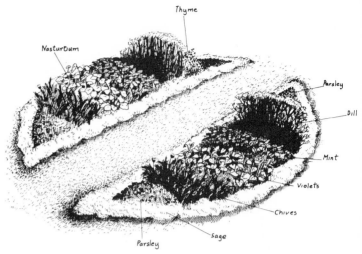

Semi-formal herb garden for a small landscape faces two ellipses across a path of grass. Contained by a low-clipped hedge of sage, numerous herbs—nasturtiums, thyme, parsley, chives, violets (for candying), mints, and dill—thrive in quantities large enough to supply all culinary needs as well as plenty of materials for drying.

Woolly thyme is one of the herbs most often used as ground cover. Its low growth makes it ideal for use between cement blocks and stepping-stones, and it stands up well to being walked on occasionally.

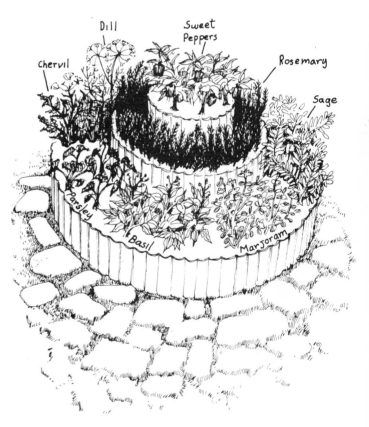

Three-tiered circular herb garden, contained and terraced by corrugated metal, holds parsley, basil, marjoram, sage, chervil, rosemary, dill, and sweet peppers.

Thyme as a lawn material works wonderfully well in a small space where it won't get too much wear and tear.

flowers, others that have pink flowers. Woolly thyme has silvery leaves and is frequently used in blocks between patio squares and garden path blocks. Caraway thyme has pretty flowers.

Chamomile, the preferred Elizabethan ground cover, grows between 3 and 12 inches tall and has tiny, daisy-like flowers. As a lawn it can be mowed 2 or 3 times annually. When walked on, it gives off a tangy scent; it stands up to droughts and can support a lot of foot traffic, though not as much as grass.

The best of the wormwoods for ground cover is probably 'Silver Mound,' a dwarf. In full sun it makes a striking silver accent, and it fairly glows in moonlight. Cut it back in spring to thicken the growth.

Sweet woodruff, which has long creeping stems and tiny flowers that appear at the tips of branches in spring, is another excellent ground cover. Grown in shaded, cooler areas, the plant generally requires soil with more humus content than many of the other herbs. It will form a dense mat in time and provides lots of fragrant cut material to dry for use in perfumes. Choose this herb as a ground cover for places under trees and along shaded paths.

Prostrate rosemary grows flat along the ground and roots as it grows. Exceptionally well adapted to the seashore, the bloom in

Wormwood—in the variety called 'Silver Mound'—makes a striking silvery accent and does beautifully in full sun even in poor dry soil. The white leaves are finely cut and offer a pretty contrast to the yellow flowers produced in late summer and early fall.

Sweet woodruff grows in cool, shady places and in spring produces tiny flowers. This herbal ground cover spreads rapidly. The crushed leaves have a flower reminiscent of vanilla.

Pennyroyal *(Mentha pulegium)*

Winter savory grows well in sandy soil and makes a handsome ground cover or edging or accent plant if it is kept clipped at the beginning of the growing season. Its lilac blossoms are attractive to bees, and the leaves are a popular culinary herb.

mild climates is almost nonstop. Excellent as a ground cover between stepping-stones and along paths, superb for cascading over big stones or low walls, a single plant can cover 4 to 8 feet. Its height is about 8 inches.

Moneywort is also known as loosestrife and creeping jennie. An inch or 2 tall, it spreads rapidly. Fragrant flowers appear in June, July, and August. Golden moneywort has golden yellow leaves and makes a strikingly colorful accent in a green landscape.

Winter savory and dwarfed varieties of lavender make good ground covers of the taller sort.

Moneywort is one of the lowest-growing of the herbal ground covers. It gets to be only 1 or 2 inches tall, and spreads rapidly. Moneywort is sometimes called loosestrife or creeping jennie.

Rosemary *(Rosmarinus officinalis)*; right, prostrate rosemary

Effective Hedges

Fragrant hedges that can be trimmed every year to provide materials for dry perfumes are a delight to the herb enthusiast.

Among the best of all fragrant herb hedges are the lavenders. The foliage is gray-green on tall plants that reach 3 to 4 feet, and the wonderfully fragrant flowers grow on spikes 12 inches long. Lavender buds are the back-

Lavender (Lavandula vera)

bone of the potpourri recipe and are a prime ingredient of sachets and moth repellents as well. Dwarf varieties grow to only 18 inches tall. Lavender is an evergreen and has needlelike leaves.

Rosemary in upright forms is a good hedge plant. It will grow 6 feet tall in warm areas, and makes a high, broad hedge if sheared annually. The gray-green foliage has a strong piney scent. In mild climates soft lavender-blue flowers appear through winter and into early summer. In cooler regions it blooms in early spring.

Lavender cotton is another fragrant hedge plant. Its height at maturity is between 18 and 24 inches, and it clips readily to the soft mounded or rounded form ideal for knot gardens. Its coral-like branching and unusual pale color make it a good choice where a strikingly different hedge is wanted.

Herb Gardens in Containers

Herbs grow well in containers. You can use anything from recycled tin cans to handsome strawberry jars. Great big plants—bay laurel, for instance—require cement urns or large wooden tubs. Small shrubby plants do well in wooden planters, large plastic pots, or ceramic planters. If yours are to be moved indoors for the winter, keep the size of the container portable. Hanging baskets make ideal homes for any number of herbs, including basil, marjoram, thyme, chives, and parsley. Those that normally grow upright will tip over and bloom down the sides of the baskets. Geraniums and nasturtium in prostrate forms are basket plants to start with.

Window boxes make ideal planting sites for a handful of the culinary herbs—dill, parsley, chervil. Mixed with scented-leaved geraniums and prostrate rosemary, these window-box herbs make handsome adornments for the house.

Containers for the herbs must meet the requirements of containers for all other plants—and then some. All potted plants have moisture problems, and because of the nature of the soil in which herbs grow, the problems are accentuated. Herbs must have good drainage, so line the bottom of the container with several inches of coarse gravel. Use a potting mixture that drains readily: for instance, 1 part spaghum moss, 1 part vermiculite, 1 part perlite, and 1 part garden soil. Keep an eye on herbs growing in containers daily for signs of lack of moisture. In really hot dry stretches of the summer, they may need to be watered daily. When planting herbs in containers, group them according to water requirements.

Scented-leaved geranium grows happily in a hanging basket. Many of the herbs grow well in this type of airy container, and make it possible to put herbs into the landscape even when there's no land. Other herbs that grow well in baskets include basil and chives, and many of the perennials such as thyme and prostrate rosemary.

Geraniums of all sorts, including the scented-leaved types used for culinary flavoring and for dry perfumes, grow in almost any container, and are especially striking here in the hollow of featherrock, a rock that has the quality of holding moisture.

Tree-form rosemary, developed from an upright form of this herb, shows the versatility of this fragrant and useful plant. Any woody or semi-woody herb can be trained to tree-form by keeping lower branches clipped as the plant shoots up.

If nothing else is handy, grow your herbs in a pail. Here, a sweet pepper plant thrives in a humous potting mixture in a sunny corner of a small city balcony.

Humidity is not as important to indoor herb plants as it is to other indoor plants, as mentioned before, with the exception of a handful whose needs for humidity are noted in the "Dictionary of Herbs." Water only when the plants are dry, and mist the plants only every week or two. It is a good idea, however, to set the herb pots on a bed of gravel to keep some water—but not a lot—in the bottom of the growing tray.

Though most herbs seem to ward off pests, when you bring potted herbs indoors you may bring with them the potential for the development of white flies, aphids, and of course, red spider mites, which thrive in the conditions herbs prefer—dryness and heat. If you find any of these on your plants, use a weak dose of malathion on nonculinary herbs, and a weak solution of yellow naptha soap as a wash for the culinary herbs.

Growing Herbs Indoors

Parsley, chervil, basil, hot peppers, caraway—almost any of the herbs listed as an-

Recycled tin can holds a whole clump of chives. This versatile herb will grow almost anywhere (as long as there's some sun) and in almost anything. Frequent cutting encourages prolific growth. The dryish pink flowers of chives are edible and make pretty garnishes for summer soups and salads.

Herbs can be started or grown indoors or on sunny balconies right in the heart of the city. Here Mary Peter, a USDA employee, shows off a garden that includes chives as well as a handful of popular vegetables—including lettuces and tomatoes.

nuals—will flourish for a time on sunny windowsills.

The perennials almost all grow indoors, though a bay tree may not fit handily into the living room. Among the best perennials and biennials for indoor growing are chamomile (under lights), rosemary, pineapple sage, santolina, woodruff and wormwood, the mints, scented-leaved geraniums, oregano, sage, southernwood, tarragon, costmary, fennel, lavender, lemon verbena, marjoram, lemon balm, catnip, rue, lavender cotton, winter savory, thyme. I have not grown all of them indoors, but other writers report success in varying degrees with all of these and many lesser-known herbs not listed here.

In selecting herbs for indoor gardens, search out dwarf forms and color and texture differences in the leaves.

Most of the herbs require at least 5 hours, and preferably more, of sun. Those noted as growing well enough in semi-sun or in semi-shade in the "Dictionary of Culinary and Fragrant Herbs" (Part IV) can do with less sunlight.

Winter Savory (*Satureja, montana*)

A collection of indoor mints shows the versatility of this sharply-scented herb. When planning an indoor herb garden, look for varied forms of your favorites, and grow them together as a group under fluorescent lights, or in a sunny window.

Geranium (Scented) (Pelargonium citriodorum)

Oregano (Origanum)

Sage *(Salvia horminum)*

Marjoram (Origanum marjorana)

Sage *(Salvia officinalis)*

Tricolor Sage

Lemon Verbena (Lippia citriodorata)

Lemon Balm (Melissa officinalis)

Mint (Orange) (Mentha citrata)

Mint (Pineapple) **(Mentha rotundifolia)**

If you really want to go in for an indoor herb collection, consider investing in an artificial light garden. To create a light garden you need fluorescent fixtures of the type sold commercially under trade names such as Gro-Lite. The heart of the fixture is a standard industrial preheat fixture with two 48-inch 40-watt bulbs. One tube should be daylight, and the other a natural white light. Another combination that works is one day-

Herbs grown indoors under fluorescent lights. Each of the three tiered shelves is 2 feet by 4 feet, and each is lighted by two 40-watt fluorescent lamps. Each shelf holds between 20 and 30 plants.

Peppermint *(Mentha X piperita)*

light tube and one plant-growth tube. You need behind the lights a reflector suspended about 18 inches above the surface of the table or stand on which the herbs are to be set. A pair of these lights will cover a garden about 2 feet by 4 feet. There are timers sold on the market that switch the lights on and off when you are absent to create whatever length of daylight your plants need—usually 16 hours total. You'll need the timer if you are going to be absent for a great number of days.

The height at which the lights are suspended above the plants is important, and so is the length of time the lights are left on. No generalization can be made on the subject, but length of lighting and height of lighting depend on the response of the plants. If there is too much light, or if the lights are too close to the plants, or left on too long—the plant leaves will bunch and sometimes brown, as though burned. If there's not enough light time, the plants grow tall, pale green stalks with spaced-out leaves, instead of close-together leaves. Experiment, beginning with 16 hours of light, and the light fixture about 18 inches above the plants—or follow suggestions included in the instructions with the light fixture you buy. Raise or lower the lights, and lengthen or shorten the time they are left on until the plant responds. What you are looking for with most of the indoor herb plants is a set-up that gives you low-growing, bushy plants whose leaves have a rich color, and which bloom in their season. You will have greater control and success than with the varying seasonal light coming through a window.

PART II
Planting and Propagating the Herbs

5 Growing Herbs from Seeds

The most popular herbs are offered as seeds or plants by catalogs and in many garden centers and nurseries (see list in the Appendix). Buy plants of those species that are slow to grow and slow to germinate, or of which you want only one plant. Start from seeds any of which you will want a quantity for use as ground cover or because you are planning to grow dozens for a special use. For herbs that transplant badly, notably dill, it is best to seed outdoors directly in the spot in which they will grow. You can start them indoors to get ahead of the season, but sometimes the check in growth which occurs when the seedlings are transplanted to the open garden makes them slower to mature than if they had been started in the open garden in the first place.

Seeds for most of the herbs should be sown after the soil and the weather have warmed. Most are not really cold weather plants. "After the soil has warmed" means when the soil has lost its winter wetness. "When the air has warmed" means after the temperature is approaching a steady 70° during the day.

Remember when selecting an outdoor site for the herb garden that the soil for most herbs must be well drained, light, and with just enough humus to keep it from drying out too quickly under summer sun. Heavy, clayey soil is not good for most herbs. To prepare the soil for an herb bed, incorporate as much sand as is needed to make it crumble readily when damp. If the soil won't ball when gathered between your two hands, that means there's too much sand and that it needs humus, such as peat moss or compost.

A number of the herbs require a sweet soil, and most of them prefer soil on the sweet side. Send a sample of your soil to your local Agricultural Extension Service for analysis, and ask that the report include suggestions for additions to the soil that will make it suitable for the growing of herbs. Liming soil is the common way to sweeten it. Bone meal is a slow-release fertilizer that sweetens soil. Dried manure and other fertilizers, except perhaps sheep manure, tend to acidify the soil, so avoid these for the growing of herbs.

Sowing Seeds Indoors

Though some of the herbs are best started as seeds outdoors, many of the perennials are slow to germinate, and will do better and grow more quickly if they are started indoors and transplanted later.

A rectangular wooden or plastic tray—the type called a flat in seed catalogs—is ideal for starting crops of herbs. Fill the flat to within ¾ of an inch from the top with potting mixture, mark off 2-inch rows, make drills in the soil with a ruler, drills about ¼ inch deep, and sow the seeds thinly in the drills. Cover with a sifting of potting soil, or with spaghum moss, or vermiculite. Water the container from beneath by placing it in a sinkful of lukewarm water, then cover the flat with plastic, loosely, and set in a warm, but not hot, room to germinate. There need be no light at this point. When the seeds have germinated, remove the plastic cover and transfer the flats to a sunny window sill or fluorescent light.

Soils for indoor growing of herbs are described in the preceding pages under "Herb Gardens in Containers."

Herbs that do not transplant well must be started in individual peat pots. Sow as described above, 3 or 4 seeds to a pot, and pull out the weakest of the seedlings as the pot becomes crowded. Seedlings growing in flats will require transfer to individual peat pots as the flats become crowded. When planting the herbs outdoors, put pot and all into the planting hole.

A planting hole for an herb pot should be about one inch deeper than the depth of the pot. Tear away the upper portion of the rim, and soak the pot well in water to which a soluble plant food such as Rapid-Gro or a vitamin hormone such as Transplantone has been added before setting it into the hole. Bring the soil up over the rim of the pot, and firm it down. Before you set the pot into the hole, fill the hole with water containing transplanting fertilizer or hormone powder.

Correct procedures for planting fragrant roses and large shrubby herbs are shown in the following photographs.

The shallow drills in a flat filled with potting mixture for the starting of herbs are made 2 inches apart and ¼ inch deep.

Peat pots are the place to start all those herbs noted as hard to transplant. Sow 3 or 4 seeds to a pot, and when they begin to crowd the pots, remove the weakest. Plant in the garden, pot and all, so as to avoid disturbing plant roots.

Bone meal is added to planting hole for a potted rose. This is a slow-release fertilizer that will feed the perennial bush for many months to come.

Mix the bone meal well into the soil at the bottom of the hole. Roses and other large perennial shrubs need loose soil at the bottom of the planting hole to encourage rapid development of new root systems after transplanting.

To remove a pressed cardboard container, slice straight down the side and around the bottom, then peel away the pressed cardboard to leave the roots free. Peat containers can be buried with the plant.

Hole of shrub to be transplanted should be several inches wider and deeper than the root system so that the plant is surrounded by a lot of loose, well-worked soil, which will encourage the development of new roots.

Plant shrubby perennials at a depth that creates a saucer effect, and brings rainwater to the plant instead of spilling it away from the plant.

Fill the planting hole with soil, and tamp it firmly with your feet. Air pockets around root systems can harm the plant and will encourage cave-ins of nearby soil when the plant is watered.

After planting, water thoroughly. Lack of water is a prime cause of failure of newly planted shrubs and trees. Water every few days the first season until new growth indicates the shrub is well established.

6
Other Ways of Propagating

Taking Tip Cuttings

Many of the herbs can be multiplied by dividing—by taking tip cuttings, for instance. The ways in which each herb can be propagated are noted in the "Dictionary of Herbs" under individual entries.

The length of a tip cutting should be 4 to 6 inches. Select tips that are flexible and light in stem color—this usually indicates recent growth, growth that will root readily. Old woody branches sometimes are less ready to sprout roots. Strip the lower leaves from your tip cuttings, and set the ends either in water or in firmly packed damp sand, on a sunny window sill. I usually let tip cuttings "rest" for 2 or 3 days in a semi-shaded corner before setting them in sunlight. Cuttings of most kinds of herbs will root within 7 to 10 days, depending on the season. Tip cuttings can be rooted for most of the herbs at almost any time of the year, but I find they develop roots most quickly at that season that is to them "early spring" in their native land, the season of major growth. In spite of that, a lot of the herbs will root quickly at summer's end and in early fall.

Tip cuttings rooted in sand should be kept partially covered by plastic and preferably set outdoors in a warm sunny spot. Lift the plastic cover during the hottest part of the day. In 10 days to 2 weeks, pull gently on the cuttings: If they resist, rooting has begun. When they truly resist lifting, they are rooted, and ready to transfer to containers filled with potting mixture, or into the open garden.

Dividing to Multiply

"Root division" describes the process exactly. Many of the herbs can be multiplied by pulling apart healthy growing clumps, usually toward the end of the growing season.

Dig the clump, and with your hands, gently, gently, tug the clump apart. You'll retain most soil around each section of the root if you plan to divide on a day when the soil is somewhat moist.

Plant each division in a prepared planting hole, or in a container filled with potting mixture, water well, and firm the soil gently around the plant. Keep the divisions moist until the plants show they are established by putting forth new growth.

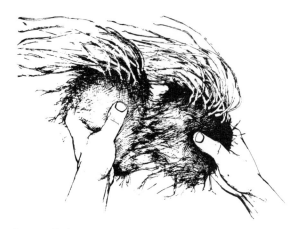

In root division, the trick is to pull the dug-up clump apart gently enough so that few of the roots are torn and little of the soil is lost.

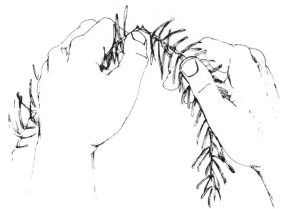

Steps in preparing to root a tip cutting: Choose young, flexible growth that shows lighter coloring than other, older stems. Break stem off at between 4 and 6 inches, and strip away lower leaves so that whatever portions of the stem are below the water surface (if rooting in water) or below the soil (if rooting in sand) will not have decaying organic matter. Next step is to place prepared cutting in a glass of water or in firmly-packed damp sand with a plastic covering.

Layering

Many of the perennials can be rooted by "layering." Rosemary in the prostrate form is typical. Long flexible stems creep along the soil, and here and there at nodes in the stems, put down young roots and establish a whole new plant.

You can do the layering if your plant does not.

Herbs suited to this way of propagation are those with stems flexible enough to readily reach to the soil and several inches beyond. Clear the soil at the base of the plant, select the branch to be layered, bend it gently to the soil, and an inch beyond the spot where the stem touches the soil, make a slight wound in the covering of the stem with a sharp knife. Dig a hole, bury the wound in the hole, and peg the wounded place on the stem into place, as shown in the illustration here. Cover the buried stem, but allow the end of the stem to stay above ground. After weeks, or sometimes months, the stem will put out roots. Dig it up occasionally to check on root growth. When growth has begun, bury the stem again and allow it several weeks, or a whole season to establish itself firmly. Then cut the stem from the parent branch, and transplant the new plant.

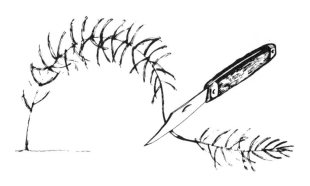

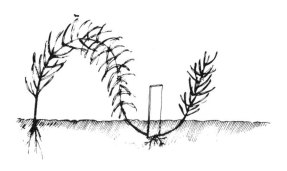

Two steps in ground-layering herbs: select and wound a long, flexible stem or branch, one long enough to reach to the soil line and beyond the foot of the plant; then bury the wound, stripped of leaves, peg it to keep it in place, fill the hole with soil, and allow the remaining tip end of the branch to stick up in the sunlight.

PART III
Using Your Herbs

7 Harvesting Herb Leaves and Branches

Once an herb plant is established, you can pick tips of branches and leaves as needed. Picking tips is a form of pruning that forces the plant to develop lateral branches along the main stems. The end result is a bushier, bigger plant. "Once the plant is established" means once it has grown 2 or 3 inches and is showing new growth. Once the plant is mature—full size—you can pick from it as much as you need. You won't harm the plant in any way unless you strip it completely of leaves. When you want a lot of one particular herb—for instance, lots of basil for *Pesto*—take equal quantities of leaves and branch tips from all the plants, instead of taking most of them from a single plant.

When to Harvest Herbs

There is a right time and a wrong time to harvest herbs. The fragrance of the herbs is in the essential oils the leaves, and sometimes the stems as well, contain. These oils are volatile. When the sun pours down on them at noon, the herb garden is at its most fragrant. That's because the sun is volatizing the herb oils and the air actually is filled with invisible drops of essential oils. The plant's store of essential fragrant oils is somewhat less after the heat of the day. Therefore, the best time to pick herbs is before the sun becomes hot in the middle of the day, but after the night's humidity has gone from the garden.

In mid- or late summer, depending on the herb, cut annuals back to the ground and freeze or dry the leaves. Cut perennials back by a third, or fill your needs by pruning the shrubs to attractive shapes—but don't cut back by more than a third of the growth. A rule of thumb which can't be applied to all the herbs is that the fragrance is strongest just before the flowers come into bloom. It can't apply to all the herbs because some bloom almost all summer long.

Drying

On a big, clean surface indoors, spread the cut herb branches and sort them into piles of the same kind. Remove any damaged leaves. If the herbs are absolutely clean, have never been spattered by mud, I feel it isn't necessary to wash them before setting them to dry. If you prefer to wash those you will use for culinary exploits, rinse them quickly under the sink spray, or swish them through cold water, and spread them on lots of paper to dry. Let them dry completely. Then spread the herbs one layer deep on screens, preferably nylon screens. Set the screens in a sunless, airy, warm room—the attic, for instance—for 10 days or 2 weeks.

With longer-stemmed herbs, such as sage, an alternate drying method is to tie the stems loosely together and to hang them in bunches upside down from a clothesline, in a warm, dark, dry place. Sunlight fades leaf and flower colors.

Storing the Herbs

When the leaves are bone dry, crackling like corn flakes, strip them from their stems into a bowl. Use a wide-mouthed funnel to pour the herbs into dry, clean containers —glass or plastic—that have tight stoppers. Label each container, and date it. Keep an eye on the interior of the containers for several days for signs of humidity. If there seems to be dampness, remove the leaves from the containers and dry again in an oven at 250° for 1 hour, repack, and seal.

Grinding and Crushing Herbs

Some herbs are used ground, or crushed, as well as whole. Herb mixes usually are ground or crushed. Prepare large "basic supply" containers of your favorite herbs in each state—whole, ground, crushed—and draw on these supplies to make up gift packages of single, or mixed, herbs, at gift-giving time.

An old herb drying shed set in a corner of a cottage herb garden.

Tansy and mint are shown hanging to dry in bunches from the rafters at Caprilands Herb Farm. Hanging behind is catnip. To dry herbs in bunches, attach them loosely at the stem ends, and hang from a nail or from a clothesline.

Harvesting herb branches and blossoms in the herb garden in the fall, when they have begun to dry naturally.

Old-fashioned herb grinder from the nineteenth century was photographed at Adelma Simmons Caprilands Herb Farm. Practical, but hard to come by today.

I crush herbs on a wooden cutting board lined with cotton. The cotton is tacked to the board with thumb tacks, the herbs are spread over the cotton, and rolled with a rolling pin. This makes a coarse grind.

To grind herbs to a finer texture I use a potato ricer, or rub the herbs through a sieve. You can crush herbs to a powder in a pepper mill—but that takes a bit of time.

Crushing herbs through a sieve is an easy way to get them just the right texture for culinary use.

8
Harvesting Herb Seeds

Many of the herbs whose seeds we use are members of the carrot family. Perhaps the most familiar relative of the carrot is Queen Anne's lace. Carrot flowers are similar in shape to those of Queen Anne's lace—delicate, wide-spreading clusters of tiny florets that make a flat flower head—and so are the flowers of many of our favorite herbs. Anise, dill, fennel, parsley are a few. Flowers of most of the herbs come into bloom toward midsummer. After the flowers have bloomed and are beginning to show signs of yellowing or browning, but before the seeds are fully ripe and the seed head dry, is the time to harvest herb seeds. Once the seeds are fully ripe, the seed head dries up and releases the seeds and you will lose them to the winds.

Use a knife or pruning shears, or kitchen shears, to cut the seed heads. Cut them an inch or two below the bottom of the flower head, and drop them into a paper bag. Or line a shallow woven basket with a kitchen towel or solid sheeting, and cut the heads into that. Dry the heads on screens lined with linen for 5 days in an airy, dark, warm room, then thresh.

Thresh your crop where there is a light breeze—outdoors or standing a little to one side of an electric fan turned to low speed. Set a big bowl on the table, and then rub the dry flower heads between your palms. The breeze will catch and carry away the fine, almost weightless, dried chaff of the flower as you crush the heads, and the heavier seeds will drop into the bowl. When you have finished threshing, gently blow away any chaff that fell into the bottom of the bowl.

Spread the seeds on a fresh cloth on your drying screens, and dry for 10 days more. If there is the slightest moisture left in the seeds when you bottle them, you run the risk of spoilage. When the seeds are completely dry, store them in small, tightly sealed containers. Check the jars for the next few days for signs of moisture, and if any appears, oven-dry the seeds for 2 hours at 250°. Label the jars, and store in a dry, dark place.

9
Drying and Storing
Herb Flowers and Branches
to Make Bouquets

The lovely old-fashioned dried flower bouquets and tussie-mussies that make exquisite gifts are created from dried herb flowers and branches (see page 40. When you are contemplating your herb harvest, plan to prepare some materials especially for bouquets. Dill or parsley flower heads on 8- to 12-inch stalks are suitable subjects, as are the flowers of chives, rosebuds, and many of the herbs listed at the back of this book. Plant a few of the flowers called everlastings—sea lavender is one of the best—especially for use in dried bouquets and tussie-mussies.

To dry branches and flowers on long stems, tie them loosely together, and hang them upside down from a clothesline in the attic or in a dry, dark room. Depending on the thickness of the flowers and stems, they will dry in about 2 weeks.

If you don't expect to make up your dried arrangements for some months, hang the herbs to dry tied loosely in brown paper bags. The bags won't prevent drying, and they will keep the plant materials free of dust and cobwebs.

Store the branches until you need them in boxes lined with tissue paper so they won't rattle around and crush when you move them. Store them in a dark, dry, warm place.

Rose buds and chive heads and violet flowers are easier to dry and use if you cut away the original stem and wire the flower heads. Use 28-gauge florist's wire cut into 8-inch lengths. Remove the flower stem, and poke one end of the wire through the center of the chive blossom until 2 inches extend above the flower head. Bend the top of the wire into a hook, and pull the hook back down through the flower until it is embedded. If you like, wrap the wire in florist's green masking tape.

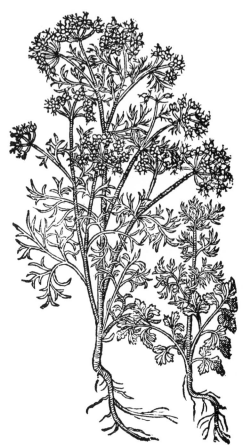

In the fall, dill has large flower heads with feathery leaves and it can be arranged in bouquets, or it can be harvested for using the seeds as seasoning.

Drying herbal blossoms to make bouquets.

10
Potpourris—Dry and Moist—for Fragrance

Potpourri is a French word pronounced po-poo-ree. A literal translation might be "fermented in a pot." And that's what makes a moist potpourri—damp, fragrant, herbaceous material fermented, usually with salt, in a pot. Its companion piece, the dry potpourri, is a mixture of fragrant herbs, flowers, spices, and other odds and ends that have been dried before they are mixed. There's no salt in most dry potpourris, and the procedure is simpler than that for moist potpourris.

What goes into a potpourri, moist or dry, is up to its creator. There's lots of room to experiment. Because the ability to detect scent and the individual response to fragrances is a very personal affair, no potpourri recipe, including the one given below, could be exactly perfect for everyone. Each potpourri-maker should feel free to heighten or tone down fragrances given in recipes according to personal preference. Another truth is that though you might follow exactly the same potpourri recipe each of two seasons, the end product could vary considerably. That is because the strength and quality of essential oils purchased from suppliers will vary, as will the fragrance of herbs and flowers, for each harvest is different, affected by soil, sun, rainfall, and ripeness. Like gardening and cooking, potpourri-making is an individual enterprise, and a recipe is only a plan, not the arbiter of the final result.

In Egypt in ancient days, potpourris were made with rose petals and biblical scents, such as myrhh and frankincense. The Greeks and the Romans found that by adding orrisroot powder to fragrant petals, they could fix the scent and make it last longer. Toward the end of the Dark Ages, potpourris began to include more of the herbs grown in cottage and monastery gardens for medicinal use, cooking, and scent. When the Western world rediscovered the spice routes to the East, spices became part of potpourri.

The most common ingredients in potpourris, moist or dry, are lots of rose petals and lavender buds and leaves—the leaves of rose geraniums, rosemary, sweet marjoram, the mints, sweet bay, lemon balm and lemon verbena, thyme, sweet basil, sweet woodruff, tarragon, and many other fragrant herbs.

To these scented materials are added spices such as cloves, cinnamon, allspice, nutmeg. Orange rind and lemon rind, cleared of white pith, stuck with whole cloves and dried, appear in many older recipes. Sometimes the dried rinds were pounded to a powder in a mortar before being included in the potpourri.

The fragrant oils in flowers and leaves fade rather quickly, and to retain them, fixatives are added to modern potpourris. Most fixatives have a fragrance of their own. Musk, civet, and ambergris were used in past centuries, but today we generally use orrisroot powder (many drugstores sell it), gum benzoin, tonka beans, oakmoss, patchouli, vetiver root, and others. To strengthen the scent further, we add essential oils. An "essential oil," the essence of a fragrance, is simply a very strong, rather oily distillation which is added drop by drop to a potpourri mixture.

You can buy these in some local pharmacies and from mail order houses that specialize in herbs and fragrances. Adelma Simmons, at Capriland Herb Farm, Silver Street, Coventry, Connecticut 06238, is one supplier, and another is the firm of Caswell-Massey Company, Ltd., 320 West 13th Street, New York, New York 10014. A list of nurseries specializing in herb plants and seeds appear in the Appendix.

Proportions for Potpourris

Tarragon (*Artemisia dracunculus*)

To create your own potpourris, as a general guideline, use the proportions below:

Rose petals: For a moist potpourri, you will need twice as many fresh petals as the potpourri will require. Drying them to the right texture for a moist potpourri reduces them by about half.

    For a dry potpourri, you will need about twice as many fresh-picked petals as the dried potpourri calls for, plus about 10 percent more. Dried to the right point for a dry potpourri, rose petals reduce by about 60 percent.

Salt: When making a moist potpourri use un- refined salt, about 1 cupful to each 3 packed cupfuls of petals.

Spices: Use about 1 tablespoonful of dried, ground spices to 4 cups of dried petals.

Fixatives: You will need about ⅓ cupful of fixative—usually orrisroot powder—for each 4 to 6 cups of petals.

Essential Oils: About 4 to 6 drops for each 6 to 8 cups of petals makes a strong fragrance. When making any potpourri, add a few drops of each essential oil at a time and make sure you want the fragrance to be stronger before you add more. Rose and lavender essential oils are those most often used.

Making a Moist Potpourri

The basic steps in making a moist potpourri are similar whatever materials are used, and once you understand these steps, you can invent your own potpourris from the materials at hand in your garden.

1. Pick twice as many rose petals as you will want. The best time to pick them is mid-morning before the sun gets hot. Dry the petals, one layer deep, on screens in a dry, dark, warm room that is well ventilated. When the bulk has been reduced by about half, they will have a leathery texture. This takes about 10 days. A leathery texture is the way petals for a moist potpourri should be before you begin the potpourri.
2. In a large earthenware or glass crock, layer the rose petals with unrefined (kosher is good) salt. Use about 1 cup of salt for every 3 packed cups of leathery rose petals.
3. Store the crock in a dark, dry, airy place where there is warmth. Stir every day or two. The contents of the crock will bubble and eventually will form a caked mass After it has caked—in about 10 days—crumble it. It is the base of the potpourri.
4. Mix dried fragrant flowers and petals, spices, herb leaves, fixatives, and essential oil into the potpourri base, seal, and cure 4 to 6 weeks in a dry, dark, well-ventilated spot.
5. Transfer the potpourri to a decorative container, one that has an airtight stopper. Keep the potpourri sealed at all times. Uncover only when you want to scent a room.

Typical Moist Potpourri Recipe

Here's a typical moist potpourri recipe you can use as a guide to create your own recipe. You need really fragrant rose petals. If not available, compensate by adding 4 to 8 drops of essence of rose—rose oil—to the finished potpourri before curing.

Moist Potpourri

9 firmly packed cups of fresh rose petals
1½ cups unrefined salt
1½ tsp. ground cinnamon
¾ tsp. ground cloves
8 dried lemon verbena leaves
½ cup dried rosemary
¾ cup dried lavender buds
½ cup orrisroot powder
1 cup dried flowers for color
4–8 drops essence of rose

1. Dry the rose petals to a leathery texture.
2. In a large crock with a wide mouth, arrange thin layers of rose petals with layers of salt, ending with a layer of salt. Put a weight, not metal, on the jar contents. (I use a flat saucer with an old iron doorstop on top.) Set the jar in a dry, dark, airy place for 10 days. Stir up the contents daily.
3. When the mixture is dry, crumble the caked portions, and mix in the remaining ingredients. Seal the jar, and cure the potpourri 6 weeks, shaking occasionally. Transfer to a decorative container. Open when you wish to scent the room.

Making a Dry Potpourri

The important difference between the moist and the dry potpourri is that the petals for a dry potpourri must be bone dry before you begin.

1. Pick twice as many rose petals, plus about 10 percent, as the recipe calls for, and set them to dry on screens in a dry, dark, warm, airy place. When they are as dry as crackly cereal, in 10 to 15 days, they are ready.
2. Combine the petals with the remaining ingredients, in a large crock with a wide mouth. Seal the crock, and store it to cure for 4 to 6 weeks, shaking occasionally.
3. Transfer the mixture to a decorative jar with a tightly fitting stopper.

Typical Dry Potpourri Recipe

Here's a recipe for a dry potpourri you can use as a guide to the creation of your own recipe. Dry potpourris in particular depend on essential oils for their fragrance, so one or more of these are usually included.

Dry Potpourri

3 cups dried rose petals

2 cups lavender buds

1 cup dried lemon verbena leaves

1 Tbs. ground allspice

1 Tbs. ground cinnamon

1 Tbs. ground cloves

Peel of 1 lemon, dried, pounded to a powder

6 drops oil of styrax

1. Combine all the ingredients in a large crock or a jar with a wide mouth. Mix in the oil 1 drop at a time, and stop when you feel the scent is strong enough. Seal, and store for 6 weeks in a dark, dry, airy place that is warm. Shake the jar contents daily.
2. Transfer to a decorative jar that has a tightly fitting lid. Open when you wish to scent the room.

11
Sachets and Scented Bags

The contents of sachets and "sweet bags" to scent linens and to keep moths from the woolens are prepared much as are potpourris. Make envelopes of decorative muslin, or coarsely woven cotton, or gather little squares of muslin or cotton into bags and tie them with wire garden ties, or pretty, narrow satin ribbons.

Because the fragrance is confined by the fabric of the bags at all times, the scents for sachets and sweet bags are usually stronger than for potpourris. Like an uncovered potpourri, a sachet will seem to lose its fragrance if left in the open air: confined in drawer and closet, however, it scents the contents, keeps insects away from the drawers, and delights you with its fragrance when you open the drawer or the door.

Devise your own sachet recipes, using this one for inspiration.

Lavender Sachet

2 cups dried lavender buds
1 cup dried thyme leaves
1 cup crushed lemon verbena leaves
1 cup dried peppermint
1 cup dried marjoram

2 cups dried fragrant rose petals
1 Tbs. ground cloves
1 cup ground orrisroot powder
4 drops essence of lavender

1. In a large crock, or a glass bowl, mix all the ingredients. Seal and cure for 4 weeks, shaking daily.
2. Divide the contents among prepared cotton or muslin envelopes. Seal the envelopes and store the sachets between piles of linens.

Herbal Moth Repellent

The main difference between a sachet and a moth repellent is in the contents. Among the most successful herbs to keep moths away are lavender, rosemary, southernwood, lavender cotton, woodruff. Spices are used, too—cloves, caraway seeds, nutmeg, mace, cinnamon, and tonka beans, and the fixative, orrisroot powder. Combined and knotted or sewn into muslin or coarsely woven cotton or linen scraps, these scents discourage pests—and do lovely things to the woolens.

Here's an old-fashioned recipe for a moth bag you can use as inspiration to devise your own.

Moth Bag

1 cup dried rose- mary	2 cups dried southernwood
1 cup dried thyme	½ cup ground cloves
1 cup dried spear- mint	

Crush together in a large bowl, and mix well. Divide among small muslin bags.

Herbal Bath Bags

These can be made from any highly scented herb: thyme, lavender, verbena, mint, marjoram, rosemary, to name a few. Prepare small cheesecloth bags, stuff them, tie them with string. Don't use discarded gift wrapping ribbons as these tend to discolor in the water.

Pick and dry leafy tips, 6 inches long, from the herbs. Combine the herbs with 2 tablespoons of rolled oats. When you are ready to run your bath, place the bag in the bottom of the tub under the faucet and turn on the hot water. When the bath is half full, swish the bag around in the water, then add cold water as needed.

Herb Lotions for the Bath

More effective and more time consuming are herb lotions for the bath. Pick 4 leafy tips from your favorite herb, and boil the tips in 2 cups of water for 15 minutes. Discard the herbs, and pour the scented water into the tub after it has been run.

12
"Strewing Herbs" and Tussie-Mussies

Herbs and fragrant grasses, dried flowers and spices were used in many ways to scent the homes of the Middle Ages. Strewing fragrant herbs through the house was a colonial custom that had its roots in man's earliest civilizations. The early Egyptians, the Greeks, and the Romans of antiquity scattered rose petals and other fragrant plant materials along streets and in banquet halls to honor guests. In the Middle Ages in Europe, floors were covered with scented rushes and dried flowers. In England and in colonial America, hyssop, lavender, rosemary, thyme, and meadowsweet along with bay leaves were hung in bunches to scent homes as well as churches and public places. The effect of the "strewing herbs" was meant to be medicinal for they believed that fresh scents purified the air.

Tussie-mussies — nosegays of herbs mixed with dried flowers — go back at least to the fifteenth and sixteenth centuries. In those days, each flower and herb had a specific meaning, one which most everyone knew. The intent of the tussie-mussie was sentimental and romantic. In colonial America, rosemary was often included in tussie-mussies, as it stood for remembrance. Pairs of herbs had special meanings: sage and chamomile stood for long life, wisdom, and patience.

Tussie-mussies are making something of a comeback today. Adelma Simmons, herb specialist and owner of Caprilands Herb Farm in Coventry, Connecticut, has been filling orders for tussie-mussies for weddings and preparing herbal crowns for brides for the last several years. The Simmons tussie-mussies include cinnamon sticks, bay leaves, rosemary, and herbal flowers symbolic of love and faithfulness and remembrance. The tussie-mussies from Caprilands Herb Farm are backed by lace doilies, and tied with ribbons. Mrs. Simmons also reports requests for sheafs of fragrant herbs and leaves for use at weddings — a return to the old custom of strewing herbs.

You can make your own tussie-mussies, and it's fun. Check the last section of the book where the herbs are listed alphabetically by common name, and find those suitable to express the sentiment you want your tussie-mussie to convey. Pick and dry the herbs you select in 8-inch branches. Wire the stems for the flowers as described on page 47, and use your imagination to find ways to wire spices and herbs: The pictures on this page illustrating the wiring of bay leaves and cinnamon sticks will suggest ways. Use 28-gauge florist wire in 8-inch lengths when making your wire stems. If you want to include big nuts, like walnuts, as "flowers," drill these and wire them. In Germany, little herb bouquets like tussie-mussies include seeds and nuts. A hazelnut, dipped in white glue, then in sesame seeds or dill weed, becomes a whole other floral affair. You can glue a circle of lentils to a nut and back them with rows of popcorn kernels and with black peppercorns, and leave your friends guessing as to the flower's horticultural origin! Or glue on exotic spices, such as the lovely large black star-shaped Chinese anise, which is most fragrant.

When all the components of the tussie-mussie are ready, poke the stems into a double lace doily, bring the lace up around the tops of the flowers and herbs, and secure the doily with long, narrow, satiny ribbons.

Caprilands Herb Farm offers its method for wiring a cinnamon stick for a tussie-mussie. Use 28-gauge florist's wire in 8-inch lengths to poke through holes made with a thin ice pick. Cinnamon-stick flowers add color and dimension to herbal bouquets.

Wire three bay laurel leaves together for the tussie-mussie.

A lacy pair of paper doilies provides the background for these tussie-mussies. Simmons begins to put together the tussie-mussie by poking sprays of dried sea lavender down into the center of the doilies.

Culinary thyme and rue are added to the tussie-mussie. Because each of the herbs has a traditional significance, such bouquets have long been used in weddings.

PART IV
Dictionary of Culinary and Fragrant Herbs

Anise (*Pimpinella anisum*)

Anise is grown for the licorice-flavored seeds, and for its leaves. If you are familiar with the flavor of fennel, or have tasted tarragon, anise leaves will remind you of either or both. You can use the leaves fresh to flavor salads. The seeds, dried, are excellent sprinkled over cookies before baking, as topping for pastries, and as flavoring for fruit pies and compotes. Start with 1/4 teaspoon and crush the seeds slightly before using to heighten the flavor. Seeds are also used on breads, in cheeses, as a flavoring for beef stews, and on baked veal and fish.

Anise is one of the oldest herbs and comes to us from the Mediterranean area and farther East. It was used as a medicine in ancient Assyria, and in the heyday of the Roman Empire, an infusion (tea) of anise seeds was offered after meals to help digestion. That may be the origin of drinks such as Anisette and Ozoo, drinks from the lands that border the Mediterranean. In the Middle Ages, anise seeds were used as a charm against bad dreams and the "evil eye," and to "unstop the liver."

Culture: Anise is an annual plant that grows to a height of between 24 and 36 inches. The plant puts out a thick mat of bright green leaves at the base and shoots up into tall stems topped by flowers that look like Queen Anne's lace. Finer leaves grow along the stems. Use the finer leaves for salads, and gather the seeds before the flower heads dry out.

Plant anise seed indoors and transfer to the outdoor garden as soon as the soil has warmed. It thrives on light soil, with lots of sand in it — that is fairly rich — and in full sun. Anise doesn't transplant well, so start the seeds in individual peat pots, and transplant pot and all to the garden.

Typical use of anise seeds for fragrance is illustrated in this potpourri recipe.

Anise

Potpourri with Anise Seeds

12 cups of fragrant
   rose petals
1 cup unrefined
   salt
1 cup fine salt
2 Tbs. ground cin-
   namon
2 Tbs. ground nut-
   meg

2 Tbs. ground
   clove
⅓ cup fresh ginger
   root, sliced
4 Tbs. anise seeds
⅔ cup powdered
   orrisroot
4 drops rose oil

1. Dry the rose petals to a leathery texture.
   Mix coarse and fine salt, and layer petals
   ½ inch deep with salt. Store in a dry,
   dark, airy place for 10 days, and stir daily
   till moist potpourri base has formed.
2. Mix in the remaining ingredients. Seal
   the jar and cure for 6 weeks. Turn into
   decorative containers.

Basil (*Ocimum basilicum*)

There are several types of basil grown in modern gardens. The one grown for culinary use has green leaves, and is called sweet basil. Use it fresh in salads, and fresh or dried in cooking Mediterranean dishes. You will find it called for in recipes for pizza, spaghetti sauce, and everywhere tomatoes are used. Basil vinegar is a delight, and the dried leaves are used in potpourris. If you like basil, use it to flavor soups, meat stews, with peas, zucchini, green beans, and cucumbers. Use ½ teaspoon fresh, minced, or ¼ teaspoon, dried, to begin with, and add more if you like. Where recipes from India call for mint, try basil instead.

A member of the mint family, basil is a native of India. In India it once was planted around homes and temples to ensure happiness, and young Italians once wore a sprig of basil to indicate that they were in love. A seventeenth-century herbalist said, "The

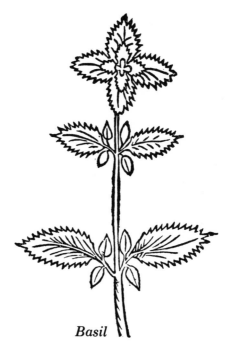

Basil

smell of Basil is good for the heart and the head, and maketh a man merry and glad." In the language of the tussie-mussie, basil stands for love.

Culture: An annual, basil grows to be 12 to 24 inches tall. Garden centers offer started seedlings, but you can grow your own indoors from seed started several weeks before the weather warms for planting. The type called sweet basil is bright green and develops small spikes of florets at the end of short stems if the plant isn't pinched out. Keep it pinched once it is a few inches tall to encourage branching. The ornamental variety, called 'Dark Opal,' is grown for its colorful foliage and its lavender-pink flowers. Plant basil outdoors in full sun, or semi-shade. It will grow in rather poor soil. Avoid nitrogenous fertilizers. Basil grows well indoors in a sunny window, or under fluorescent lights. Pot up healthy plants at the end of the season, and cut them back by one third, then install on a sunny sill for the winter. They'll keep going for a long time.

The recipe below is probably the most famous use of basil.

Francesca Bosetti Morris's *Pasta al Pesto*

2 cups firmly packed fresh sweet basil leaves	1 tsp. salt
	2 Tbs. pine nuts or walnut meats
	½ cup olive oil
Fresh ground black pepper to taste	½ cup grated Parmesan or Sardo cheese
3 cloves garlic, peeled and minced	Hot, buttered spaghetti for 4

1. Put all ingredients, except the cheese, into the blender. At high speed, blend, pushing basil leaves down from time to time. Add more olive oil if the contents stick. When the sauce has the consistency of whipped butter, add the cheese.
2. Mix thoroughly into hot, buttered spaghetti. (Freeze leftovers and use later for flavoring soups.)
Makes 4 portions.

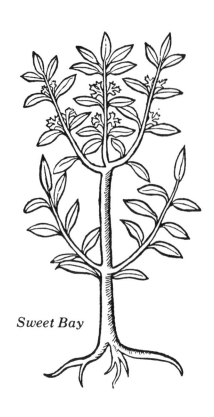

Sweet Bay

Bay Laurel (*Laurus nobilis*)

Bay leaf is a frequent condiment in European cooking, notably French, Italian, and Spanish. Along with thyme, it is used in stocks for cooking fish, in fish soups and chowders, in meat stews, marinades for game, spicy vegetable hors d'oeuvres, and in pickles. Add 1 large leaf only to a recipe for 6 or 8, and add when you begin the cooking. Discard the leaf when cooking is finished. Dried bay leaves are used in potpourris and tussie-mussies.

There are almost more legends about bay laurel than about any other herb. According to Greek mythology, the bay laurel was once a lovely nymph running from the god, Apollo. To save her, the gods turned her into the bay laurel, and so the leaves have been a symbol of victory every since. The word "baccalaureate" comes from bay laurel, and "winning your laurels" refers to the crowns of bay leaves victors were awarded in both Greece and Rome. In the language of the tussie-mussie, bay laurel stands for glory. In the Middle Ages, a powder made of bay berries was used to improve the complexion and it had many other medicinal and culinary uses.

Culture: An evergreen tree from the Mediterranean region, bay laurel grows in warm regions of this country as a small tree or a large shrub. It can be trained to a pyramidal shape or a round-headed form, makes a good hedge plant or tubbed specimen for mild climates or the greenhouse. The leaves are stiff, about 4 inches long. Greenish white flowers are followed by black berries. In the north, bay laurel can be grown indoors in winter and set outdoors for the warm weather.

Buy bay laurel as a plant. Grow it in full sun, in well-drained, slightly acid soil that isn't too fertile. Pick leaves any time for use as needed.

Use of bay leaf in pickling is illustrated in this old-fashioned recipe for sweet pickles.

Borage

Sweet Pickles with Bay

25 small gherkin cucumbers	1½ tsp. whole cloves
1 quart boiling water	1½ tsp. celery seeds
½ cup salt	1½ tsp. mustard seeds
1½ quarts white vinegar	1 stick cinnamon, broken
1 pint water	2 bay leaves, crushed
1½ tsp. allspice	1½ cups sugar
1½ tsp. peppercorns	

1. Wash cucumbers and drain. Place in a large crock. Combine boiling water and salt and pour over the cucumbers. Let stand overnight. Drain.
2. Combine the remaining ingredients in an enamel kettle. Heat to boiling. Add cucumbers to the kettle, and return the contents to a boil.
3. Pack the cucumbers at once into sterile glass jars, then fill the jars with pickling liquid and seal
4. Let stand 4 weeks or longer before using.

Borage (*Borago officinalis*)

Borage leaves have a flavor like cucumbers, and are used in pickling, in cooling summer drinks, and in salads. The lovely, star-shaped blue flowers are sometimes used as garnishes in iced drinks and to decorate cakes and summer desserts. Dried, they are used in bouquets.

While borage isn't the most used of all the herbs, it does have a romantic place in the history of herbs. In the tussie-mussie, it stands for courage, and medieval herbalists believed it brought cheer to those who ate the leaves or swallowed drinks garnished with the flowers. It was used as a cure for abscesses, and fevers, and eaten as a boiling green. The fresh leaves were combined in salads with mint, sage, parsley, garlic, fennel, and rosemary.

Culture: Plant borage for its gray-green leaves and for its pretty blue flowers. It is an annual herb that can be started from seed outdoors any time after the temperature has warmed. It doesn't transplant easily, so if you start it indoors, place the seeds in individual peat pots and transplant pot and all to the garden. Borage grows to be from 18 to 36 inches tall, and prefers full sun. It thrives in soil supplied with sand, and not overly fertile. You can grow borage as a container plant on the terrace and patio.

The recipe below indicates how borage is used in salads.

Tomato Salad with Borage

4 very ripe red tomatoes	1 small garlic clove, peeled
½ sweet green pepper	½ tsp. salt
½ Bermuda onion, peeled	4 Tbs. olive oil
1 small head Boston lettuce	1 Tbs. mild vinegar
	¼ cup borage leaves, minced
	Salt to taste

1. Peel the tomatoes and cut into wedges. Mince the pepper and onion. Wash, drain, dry the lettuce, and chill everything.
2. In a wooden salad bowl, crush the garlic with the salt. Add the olive oil and vinegar. Put the chilled tomatoes in the dressing, and mix well. Sprinkle with borage leaves. Toss just before serving. Serves 4 to 6.

Caraway (*Carum carvi*)

Though caraway is an exceptionally useful culinary herb, not many people grow it. In Northern European cooking, the seeds are sprinkled on everything from cheese, green beans, beets, carrots, cabbage, potatoes, to rye bread, cakes, cookies, and applesauce. Crushed, the seeds add wonderful flavor to dips and spreads, sauerbraten and pork dishes, goose, and to melted butter sauces for noodles or macaroni. Caraway is used commercially as a flavoring agent for the German liqueur, Kummel. Try ½ teaspoon of

the seeds, whole or crushed, before adding more to a recipe.

Roman soldiers are believed to have brought caraway from its home in Asia Minor to the West. It has been popular ever since. Medieval feasts often ended with "caraway comfits," and it was believed "good for the stomach," "warming," and a remedy for restoring "hair where it has fallen away." In those days, the root was cooked and eaten.

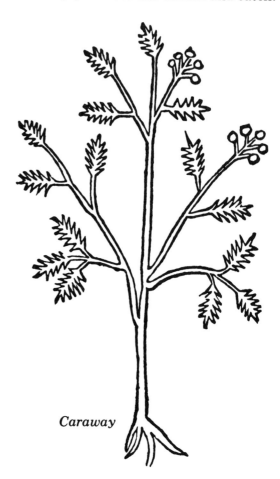

Caraway

Culture: Caraway is a hardy biennial, a plant that returns the second year, but dies at the end of that season. It often sows itself, and grows to about 30 inches. Since the seeds are the crop, and the plants flower only the second season, to have a continuous supply, you must replant caraway every year. The seedlings will grow the first year, and the flowers, followed by seeds, will appear the second year. A member of the parsley family, the caraway flowers resemble the flat, green seed heads of that popular herb. Sow seeds indoors a few weeks before planting weather, and transplant pot and all to the garden when the weather has warmed. Plant in full sun in a neutral soil that has lots of sand for good drainage.

The vinegar recipe below can be used to make other herbal vinegars.

Vinegar with Caraway

2 Tbs. caraway   1 pint white vinegar
seeds

1. Mash the seeds in a glass bowl. Heat the vinegar almost to boiling. Pour over the seeds, stirring and mashing with a wooden spoon. Pour into a pint jar, cover, and let stand in a warm room for 10 days. Shake the jar daily. Taste at the end of 10 days. If not flavorful enough, strain out the seeds, and replace with fresh, crushed seeds. Cover again, and let stand 5 more days.
2. Strain through a fine sieve and store in a clean pint jar.

Catnip (*Nepeta cataria*)

This is an herb to grow if you love cats. They seem irresistibly drawn to it, whether growing in the garden, fresh from the garden, or dried and sewn into little cotton bags or scratching posts.

Some medicinal effects were once claimed for catnip. In the last century, it was made into tea, and swooning ladies said it relieved both headaches and hysteria.

Culture: This is a hardy perennial that will go wild if you aren't careful. The plants are large, 3 to 4 feet tall, straggly, and look like a less green mint. Catnip grows best in full sun, in rich soil that has enough organic matter to retain humidity. Sow the seeds in mid-spring. They germinate in about 10 days. Or plant root division, or rooted stem cuttings. To make stem cuttings, cut 8-inch tips and set in damp sand in a sunny window. Cuttings planted in early spring will be

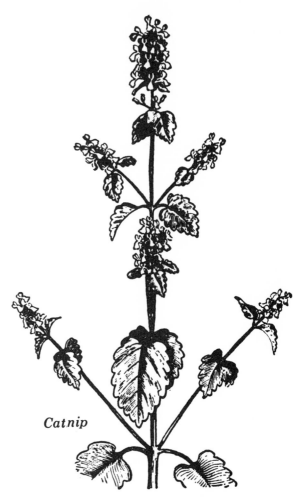

Catnip

established soon enough for you to take tip cuttings just before the flower buds begin to open in midsummer.

Chamomile (*Anthemis nobilis*)

A charming little herb that is grown in mild areas as a ground cover, chamomile gives off a slight fragrance when walked on. Today, its primary use as an herb is in soothing teas and in hair preparations. The flowers, cut and dried, are used to make a rinse that does seem to brighten dull hair. It is also used in dry perfumes.

In a tussie-mussie, chamomile's statement is one of meekness and patience. Sometimes called "ground apple," it was grown in the medieval garden as a ground cover and as a

Chamomile

Chamomile Hair Rinse

½ cup dried cham-
omile flowers

4 cups water

Boil together for 5 minutes. Strain. Apply to the hair after washing.

Herbal Shampoo with Chamomile

1½ cups boiling
water
2 Tbs. dried rose-
mary
2 Tbs. dried cham-
omile flowers

¼ cup dried mint
leaves, crushed
1 egg
¼ tsp. borax
2 cups nondeter-
gent shampoo

1. Pour boiling water over the herbs in a medium bowl, cover, and allow the herbs to steep for 1 hour. Remove the herbs.
2. Beat the egg until frothy, and beat into the shampoo, along with the borax. Combine with the herbal infusion. Bottle, and keep stored in the refrigerator. It will keep about 1 month. Use as regular shampoo.

Chervil (*Anthriscus cerefolium*)

If you have a small herb garden, and are growing parsley, you may not want to make room for chervil, which is similar in flavor, and used much as is parsley. The flavor has a hint of tarragon in it, however, and is prized by gourmet cooks. Use it fresh, or dried, in salads, stuffings, sauces, omelets, seafood, and cheese dips. Use it as a substitute for parsley in cooking stews and casseroles and fish dishes. It is excellent, too, in sorrel salad, and spinach soup. Use ½ teaspoon minced fresh with root vegetables after they have finished cooking.

Chervil was first recorded in Roman history about 2,000 years ago but doesn't seem to have built up a body of folklore as have other herbs. Herbalists considered it useful for digestion, and it was chopped up in "Sallets" (salads) in England. Chervil also was used as a compress for wounds.

Culture: A small plant that grows as an annual, chervil often self-sows if allowed to go to seed, so that next year's garden may

cover for mounded earthen seats. A tea of chamomile was taken for headaches and it was boiled with honey and applied as a complexion aid. Fresh chamomile flowers were boiled with orange peel to "make a water for washing the hands at table."

Culture: Chamomile lawns can't be played on but they can be walked on. A perennial, and evergreen, chamomile grows into a fuzzy green plant about 3 inches tall in early spring. It will grow up to 12 inches — at which point it blooms — unless mowed. The flowers are tiny and look like daisies.

Sow seeds in early spring or mid-fall, in moist, well-drained soil supplied with lots of organic matter. Chamomile will grow in sun or semi-shade. Once the seeds have sprouted, the plants will multiply themselves by underground runners. You can dig a clump and start a new stand elsewhere anytime after early summer.

Below are some cosmetic preparations for the hair that show how chamomile is used.

Chervil

1. Wash, drain, tear into bits all the lettuce, and chill.
2. Just before serving, toss the greens with the dressing, the garlic, and when well-coated, toss with the minced chervil.

Chervil Herb Mixture for Egg Dishes and Chicken

1 tsp. dried summer savory	1 tsp. dried basil
1 tsp. dried tarragon	1 tsp. dried chives
1 tsp. dried chervil	1 tsp. dried rosemary

Crush all the herbs together, and store in a tightly capped bottle. Use 1 teaspoonful to flavor omelets or chicken dishes.

Chives

bring lots of volunteers. The plants grow to be 6 to 12 inches tall, and can be used alternately with parsley plants as edging for low borders. Sow seeds in full sun, or partial shade, but do not cover with soil. Tamp firmly. Seeds will germinate in about 7 days. Soil for chervil should be moderately rich.

The two recipes below indicate the proportions of chervil used in salads and in herb mixtures.

Green Salad with Chervil

1 medium head iceberg lettuce	1 clove garlic, peeled and minced
1 small head Bibb or Boston lettuce	3 Tbs. fresh chervil, minced or 1½ Tbs. dried
1 heart of escarole	
¾ cup Oil and Vinegar Dressing	

Chives (*Allium schoenoprasum*)

Chives are oniony in flavor, and one of the most attractive and useful of all the herbs. The chopped stems, slim, hollow tubes, are used in soups, notably Vichyssoise, to flavor baked fish, in salads, in sour cream or cheese dips, and anywhere that a light onion flavor is appropriate. The flowers, which are dry-ish and purple-pink in color, can be eaten. Use them as garnishes for soups, aspics, and most any cool dish you want to dress up. The stems, blanched 30 seconds, are used as garnishes for aspics and other molded dishes. Freeze chopped chives in sealed plastic bags and use as needed. Or chop and dry chives and store in tightly capped bottles: the color and flavor are better if they are frozen.

Chinese chives, *Allium tuberosum,* is a decorative species that bears white flowers. It grows to be about 18 inches tall, and has a flavor that seems to include garlic as well as onion.

Though chives have been used for thousands of years in cooking, there seems to be little history associated with the plant in most herbal sources. Onions have so long been a part of man's food that perhaps oniony herbs lost their mystery before the herbalists started writing.

Culture: Chives grow in small clumps of reedlike stems, from seed or from bulblets that resemble onion sets or garlic cloves. They reach 12 to 15 inches in height and are perennials hardy to −25° or below. They grow best in rich, moist soil, well supplied with organic matter. Set in sun or partial sun. Chives grow beautifully in containers outdoors, and indoors too. Use them as edgings for small flower borders. One of the endearing qualities of chive plants is the speed with which they replace stems as you cut them. The flowers develop in summer as clusters above the tops of the stems. Keep them picked to keep the plant producing vigorously. Or allow the flowers to go to seed, harvest the seeds, and start a new clump in flats indoors.

Most garden centers and many grocery stores in spring sell potted chives. Before setting out, divide each clump in four.

This recipe is for the soup that can't do without chives, Vichyssoise. The Vinaigrette recipe below is a classic use of chives, a very sharp sauce made green by chives and served with cold leftover meat or vegetables.

Vichyssoise

2 Tbs. butter	3 cups old pota-
1 small onion,	toes, peeled and
peeled and sliv-	diced
ered	Salt to taste
5 large or 8 small	1 cup heavy cream
leeks, washed	4 Tbs. chives,
and chopped	chopped
2 quarts chicken	
broth	

1. Melt the butter in a soup kettle, and cook in it the onion and the leeks. Add the stock and the potatoes, and boil rapidly until the potatoes are tender.
2. Put through the blender at low speed, 2 cups at a time, or mash through a sieve. Salt, taste, and add more salt if needed, then chill thoroughly.
3. Just before serving, add all the cream, and sprinkle with chives.
Serves 6 to 8.

Vinaigrette Sauce with Chives

2 cloves garlic,	1 shallot, peeled,
peeled	or 1 tsp. minced
1 tsp. salt	onion
½ tsp. pepper	3 Tbs. minced
1 cup olive oil	chives
½ tsp. dry mustard	2 Tbs. minced
2 Tbs. white wine	parsley
vinegar	⅛ tsp. pepper
2 Tbs. Tarragon	
Vinegar	

Process all the ingredients in the blender for 2 minutes. Chill before serving.
Makes about 1⅓ cups.

Coriander (*Coriandrum sativum*)

Coriander seeds and leaves, too, are used. The leaves are sometimes offered as Chinese parsley in Oriental food shops, and as *cilantro,* in Spanish food shops. When I lived in areas where I couldn't buy Chinese parsley (and was doing a lot of Oriental cooking), I planted coriander seeds in my indoor flower

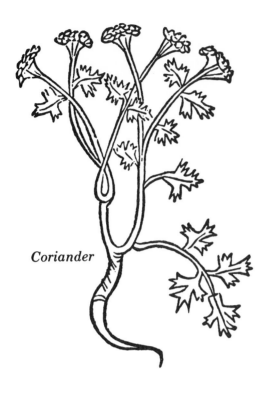

Coriander

You can start seeds indoors in individual peat pots, and transplant pot and all to the garden after the weather warms. Germination takes about 7 days. Set coriander in full sun, in soil that is moderately rich and well drained. In very hot areas it will be more successful in partial shade. Grow it on the patio in containers, or indoors on a windowsill or under lights. Harvest side leaves at will for use fresh, then allow the plant to produce flowers and set seeds for a winter crop of coriander seeds.

Coriander is an ingredient in many curries, where it is mixed with other spices, as in the recipe below.

Curry Powder with Coriander Seeds

¼ cup coriancer seeds	1 Tbs. mustard seed
2 Tbs. saffron threads	1½ tsp. red pepper, crushed
1 Tbs. cumin seed	1 Tbs. poppy seed

Grind all the ingredients together in a pepper mill, and bottle tightly.

Costmary (*Chrysanthemum balsamita*)

Costmary is an old-fashioned herb grown today primarily for use in dry perfumes. The dried leaves have a sweet, subtle fragrance, wonderful in sachets and in dried bouquets. Use the very fine tips of the fresh leaves minced in green salads.

The name, costmary, comes from the plant's association with the Virgin Mary and with Mary Magdalene. In colonial days in America, the big leaves were used as Bible markers, and the name "Bible leaf" is often used instead of costmary. In the language of the tussie-mussie, costmary stands for fidelity. In the days of Elizabeth I, costmary was called "alecost" and was brewed in beers and used to flavor sausages. It was also used as a strewing herb and to scent wash-water served after meals.

pots, and had all I needed. The seeds, whole or ground, are used in dried bean dishes, Indian and Spanish cooking, with stews and boiled fresh vegetables. One half teaspoon of ground coriander makes a whole other thing of homemade brown bread, and of baked apples. You can make coriander vinegar — an excellent change in salads — by following the recipe for Caraway Vinegar. Place one crushed seed of coriander in demi-tasse coffee and serve for gala occasions topped with whipped cream. Use coriander leaves, fresh, in salads. Coriander is also used in potpourris.

Coriander has been used along the Mediterranean since prehistoric times. Seeds have been found in tombs in Egypt, and we believe it grew in the hanging gardens of Babylon. It is referred to in the Bible, and the herbalists of the Middle Ages recommended it highly for, among other things, worms. Medicinally, it was often mixed with honey.

Culture: Coriander is an annual, related to parsley, and grows to about 18 inches tall.

Culture: This is a large, 5 to 6 feet tall, perennial herb, hardy to about −20°. It bears fragrant gray-green leaves in clumps. The leaves are large, and not especially decorative in the border, but at midday when the sun is hot, they scent the air, and you can notice their fragrance after a rain. The plant can be propagated by root division begged from a friendly garden, or you can buy potted plants at garden centers and from herb specialists. Plant in sandy soil, in sunlight, or in semi-sun. Grow it on the patio, or terrace. You won't need more than one.

The recipe for sachets below is a typical use of costmary.

Costmary Sachet for Linens

½ cup dried patchouli leaves	2 cups dried lavender buds
1½ tonka beans, ground	½ cup orrisroot powder
½ cup dried woodruff	2 drops rose oil
2 cups dried costmary	2 drops lavender oil

Crush all the ingredients, except the oils, together in a large bowl. Add the oils, drop by drop, mixing as you add. Divide the potpourri into small cotton bags and tie with string. Place among linens.

Cumin (*Cuminum cyminum*)

Cumin is an herb grown for its seed, which is used to flavor many Mexican, Indian, and Latin American dishes. Among Spanish people is it called *cominos* or comino seed. It is an ingredient in chili powder, in curries, and is excellent alone in egg dishes, soups, sauerkraut, pork, and cheese dishes. The seeds make a tasty garnish for cheese canapes and chopped egg dishes of all sorts, and a pinch of ground cumin creates a whole new dimension in roasted lamb.

This is an herb seed that predates biblical times. It appears in the Bible in Matthew 23, where Jesus says, "... ye pay tithe of Mint and Anise and Cummin...." Probably because of its great value in those days, cumin

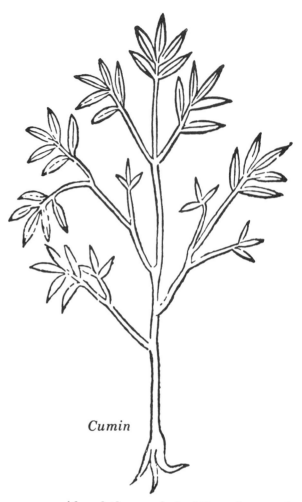

Cumin

was considered the symbol of the miser, and it was believed that a happy future lay in store for the wedding couple who carried cumin to the marriage ceremony. In the Middle Ages it was used to flavor peacock, the aristocrat of dishes, and to "destroy the wicked winds in a man's stomach."

Culture: A member of the carrot family, cumin is a small, scented annual that grows to about 6 inches high. Sown outdoors early in May, it will bloom late the following month. The flowers are small and white. Plant cumin in full sun, in well-drained ordinary garden soil, without too much fertilizer. You can start cumin indoors, too, but it grows so quickly there's not much need to. It has a taproot, and doesn't transplant easily, so start it in peat pots and transplant pot and all to the garden.

Raita, a side dish served with Indian meals, is a typical Eastern use of this herb.

Raita

2 medium cucumbers	½ tsp. salt
1 medium onion, peeled	1 tsp. ground cumin
	½ pint plain yogurt

1. On the coarse side of the grater, shred the cucumbers, and chill for 6 hours. Pour off the cucumber water, squeeze the slices dry and set in a flat serving dish.
2. Grate the onion over the cucumber, and sprinkle with salt and cumin. Mix in the yogurt, and chill 1 hour more before serving.
   Makes 8 to 10 portions.

Dill (*Anethum graveolens*)

Dill weed and dill seed are cooking herbs that come from the same plant, a tall annual with feathery foliage. The seeds are crunchy, and are used whole when texture and a sharp flavor are wanted. The more subtle leaves, called "weed" in the dried state, are used fresh or dried to flavor everything from pickles to vegetables and baked fish dishes. Use the seeds when the dish is to be cooked for a long time. Use the leaves when there will be little or no cooking. Snip fresh dill leaves into sour cream and into mayonnaise-based sauces, into dressings, salads, on cooked fish, cauliflower, with fresh green beans, carrots, parsnips.

Dill teas were once used to calm sufferers, and the foliage was considered a frustration to witches. Other references say it was used by practitioners of black magic to help them have their way. It was expected to cure "yexing" — hiccoughs — and to heal wounds. Dill water was used as a mild stomach medicine for children.

Culture: Dill is an annual herb that grows well anywhere but is difficult to transplant. Grow it in window boxes, in a sunny window indoors, or under fluorescent lights. Start the seeds indoors a few weeks before weather warms, in individual peat pots. Germination

Dill

takes about 7 days. Or sow seeds where the plants are to grow in the garden, and water well and frequently until they germinate. Plant dill in full sun, in well-drained and fairly rich soil. Keep weeds down until the plants are well established. Snip dill leaf as needed once the plants are established. Toward the end of summer, allow the plants to develop flowers — that is, don't snip off the tops — and just before the seeds ripen, cut them into a paper bag or a linen-lined basket. Cut side foliage before it browns at the season's end, and freeze sealed into plastic, or air dry and bottle.

This use of dill with potatoes suggests the use of dill with other vegetables.

Potato Salad with Dill

16 to 20 new potatoes	¼ cup chives or onions, minced
½ cup Oil and Vinegar Dressing	½ cup mayonnaise
½ tsp. coarse salt	½ tsp. mustard powder
2 cloves garlic, peeled and minced	½ cup fresh dill weed, or ¼ cup dried

1. Wash new potatoes and cook until just underdone. Drain, and cool 5 minutes.
2. With two sharp knives, slash the potatoes into halves and quarters. Pour dressing over them, sprinkle with salt, and toss with garlic and chives. Marinate at room temperature until completely cooled, tossing occasionally.
3. Toss again, this time with mayonnaise and mustard, just before serving, and sprinkle liberally with dill.
   Makes 6 to 8 portions.

Fennel (*Foeniculum,* all species)

Fennel seed, like anise seed, has a licorice flavor, and is used much in Italian cooking. Seeds or snips of the feathery foliage, called fennel weed, add a wonderful flavor to egg dishes, fish, stews, marinades for meats, vegetables, cheese, baked or stewed apples, pickles, sauerkraut, breads, cakes, and cookies. Crushed, the seeds mixed with sour cream make an intriguing cocktail dip. The seeds are also excellent sprinkled on chicken before broiling, with braised celery, sweet vegetables like yams and sweet potatoes.

Don't confuse the plant grown for fennel seed with the plant that is called sweet fennel. Sweet, or Florence, fennel is a celery-like vegetable, *Foeniculum vulgare dulche,* sold in specialty shops as *finocchio.* The fennel commonly grown for seed, *Foeniculum vulgare,* grows as tall as 5 feet. Sweet fennel is low-growing, and the base looks like celery if celery grew in a short, bulbous form. The tops of both forms of fennel, and the seeds, can be used as herbs, but *Foeniculum vulgare* is the one to select if you want to gather and store a big seed crop.

Fennel has long figured in Meditteranean

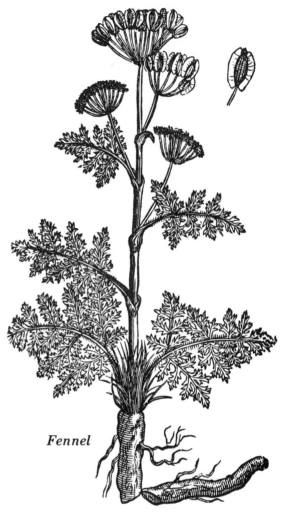

Fennel

cooking, and even in ancient history. The Battle of Marathon was fought in a field of fennel, and the word marathon is the Greek word for fennel. According to the American Spice Trade Association, fennel was considered a sacred herb, and was used to ward off many kinds of disease. In the language of the tussie-mussie, it stands for flattery. Medieval herbalists recommended fennel for mistiness of the eyes, worms in the ears, and to "break the dropsy, and all manner of swelling."

Culture: Grow sweet fennel in warm regions because it has a long enough season to develop the bulblike base and because while the base is growing, you can use fresh foliage for flavoring. Cut and dry the foliage and seeds that may develop in the flower head before harvesting the base. To blanche the vegetable base so that it will look like the sweet fennel sold in specialty shops, hill the soil around the base as soon as it reaches the size of a large egg. In about 10 days, it should be ready for harvesting. Grow the taller variety as a perennial in cooler climates, and use the seeds and foliage as herbs fresh and to dry. Height of this sort is 3 to 4 feet at maturity. Plant fennel seeds in full sun after the soil has warmed. It requires good drainage, and a fertile loam.

Fennel leaf, or weed, improves any leftover vegetables, or canned vegetable, and can be used as in the recipe below.

Cold Vegetable Salad with Fennel

1 shallot, minced
1 cup Oil and Vinegar Dressing
4 to 6 cups cooked green or lima beans, peas, carrots, cauliflower, or other vegetable
1 large iceberg lettuce

1 tablespoon olive oil
2 Tbs. butter
1 garlic clove, peeled and crushed
2 slices stale bread, crustless
2 Tbs. minced fresh fennel weed, or 1 Tbs. dried

1. Blend shallot and dressing, and pour over the vegetables in a medium saucepan. Over low heat, simmer, uncovered, 3 minutes, then cover and chill with the lettuce broken into bits.
2. Heat the oil and butter in a skillet, and brown the garlic in it. Remove the garlic, and fry the bread until golden, flipping often so both sides absorb oil and butter.
3. When ready to serve, toss the vegetables and lettuce with the bread, crumbled, and garnish with fennel.
Serves 8 to 10.

Garlic (*Allium sativum*)

Garlic belongs to the genus Allium, which includes all the onions we use in cooking. It is one of the most used of all cooking herbs and appears in almost every type of cuisine from China westward. The bulb consists of

Garlic

several cloves, each sheathed in a papery covering and clinging to a central stem. Peeled and minced fresh into foods, the flavor of garlic is fairly strong and always recognizable. Added to stews or soups, sauces for spaghetti, and vegetables, at the beginning of the cooking, the flavor blends with other flavors and is much less distinct. Use garlic minced or crushed in salads and salad dressings, with raw tomato dishes, and cook it in soups, sauces, meats, poultry, fish, and in game marinades. Crush and mash with butter to make a spread for garlic bread; boil 1 clove with peas to sweeten them; crush it into prepared mustard and smear a beef roast with it. Prick lamb and poke slivered garlic into the holes before roasting. Garlic is an essential ingredient in many pickle recipes as well.

Garlic has long been associated with strength — perhaps because of the pervasiveness of its odor! There are records that show that it was eaten by Egyptian workmen at least 5,000 years ago, and even today, many Europeans claim it purifies the blood, and cleanses the body of toxic substances. Modern-day herbalists use garlic cures for various problems associated with digestion and skin.

Culture: Though garlic is cultivated in Southern gardens for commercial use, I have been able to grow it as far north as northern Vermont. Plant individual garlic cloves, from seedsmen, garden centers, or the supermarket, broad base downward, 1 to 2 inches deep in fertile, well-drained soil, in mid-spring. The bulbs will send up hollow-stem-med leaves, like those of onions or chives, which in time will develop chive-like flowers. When these are in full bloom, bend the stems in half, leave 8 to 10 days more, then dig the bulbs. Dry them in the garden for 2 or 3 days, braid the stems, and hang to dry in an airy, warm, dry room.

The recipe below is just one of countless ways garlic is used in gourmet cooking.

Garlic Butter

6 garlic cloves, minced	Salt and pepper to taste
1 cup boiling water	2 Tbs. fresh pars-
½ cup soft butter	ley, finely minced

1. Set the unpeeled cloves in the boiling water. Bring to a boil, and boil 5 minutes. Drain, peel, and rinse the cloves under cold water. Return to the boiling water, and allow the water to boil up once more. Drain the garlic again, and with the salt and pepper, pound it to a smooth paste in the bottom of a small bowl.
2. Beat the butter into the garlic. Use 1 teaspoon with broiled or boiled fish, with hamburgers, steaks, boiled potatoes, or to enrich sauces made with drippings from roasts.

Geranium (*Pelargonium,* all scented species)

Scented-leaved geraniums have long been used for flavoring jellies and jams and pickles, and for dry fragrances. There are many varieties of scented-leaved geraniums, but probably the most commonly available are those called rose geranium, which has lavender flowers (*P. graveolens*); lemon-scented geraniums, which have purple and lilac flowers (*P. crispum*); its relative, the variety 'Prince of Orange,' which is orange-scented; and apple-scented geranium, which has white flowers (*P. odoratissimum*). These geraniums were used much more as herbs for scent and for cooking in the last century than they are now, and it seems a pity because they are among the most decorative of all the plants for the herb garden. If you are looking for something unusual, try to find varieties of the trailing nutmeg-scented type with pink-veined white flowers, the spice-scented geraniums with pink and red flowers, the peppermint-scented geraniums whose white flowers are spotted with red. Dried leaves of the sweetly fragrant species are added to potpourris, and the leaves of the spicy geraniums are added to pickles and jams and jellies.

Culture: The geraniums can be grown indoors in cool climates, and in the open during the warm weather, either in the open garden, in containers, or in baskets. In warm regions, the geraniums are perennial and will grow outdoors almost anywhere. Sprawling types are used as ground covers, and will climb, or run down, seaside cliffs. Upright types can be trained in tree forms.

In areas where summers are exceptionally hot, plant rooted geranium seedlings where there is some shade from midday sun. In the North, locate them in south-facing settings in windows for winter, and outdoors in summer in west-to-south facing sites. In cool areas, set geraniums in the garden in their pots. Fertilize potted geraniums every two weeks. Geraniums growing in the open garden like a dry soil and one that is not too rich. Feed geraniums growing as ground cover 2 or 3 times yearly. Keep newly planted geraniums pinched back to encourage branching.

Sow geranium seeds indoors in March. Germination takes 15 to 20 days. Or propagate new plants from stem cuttings or semi-new wood. The trailing types I find root best in January, and that's the month I cut back severely hanging basket specimens I brought indoors in the fall. Trailing types and scented-leaved types seem to prefer more shade than do upright forms, and to require more watering as well.

A potpourri made with geranium leaves shows how these are used in fragrant combinations.

Progressive Potpourri Made with Geranium Leaves

2 cups unrefined salt
2 cups borax
⅓ cup ground cinnamon
5 packed cups dry geranium leaves
1 cup dried lemon verbena leaves

½ cup dried thyme
½ cup broken, dried bay leaves
1 cup dried lavender buds
6 drops rose oil
6 cups fresh, fragrant rose petals

1. Mix the salt, borax, and cinnamon in a large wide-mouthed crock. Seal and keep in warm, dry place.
2. In a separate crock, place the fragrant geranium and lemon verbena leaves, thyme, bay leaves, and lavender buds, all chopped together. Add the rose oil, seal, and store.
3. As rose petals become available, dry to leathery texture, and add to the borax mixture. Stir daily. When all the rose petals have been added, combine the two mixtures, seal, and cure 6 weeks.

Ginger Root (*Zingiber officinale*)

Ginger root is a must in Oriental cuisine, where it is used fresh, frozen, and ground. Ground, the dried root is the base for flavor in gingerbread, spice cakes, cookies. A pinch of ginger, ground, does a lot for chicken casseroles and almost any sauce. It is part of a good curry, is used in pickles and conserves, with baked or stewed fruits, vegetables, fish, lamb, beef, pork, veal, and soups. Add a little ground ginger to plain commercial may-

Ginger Root

onnaise and it improves the flavor greatly. The leaves of the ginger plant are sometimes used to flavor soups.

For ages, ginger was called a rich man's spice, and rivaled black pepper — the most valuable of spices — in price. Ginger was used in England before the eleventh century, and fancy gingerbread was a favorite of Elizabeth I's court. Spanish ships took ginger root to the Caribbean, and it is now grown in Jamaica as an export crop. And in American and English homes in the last century, ginger was not only used in potpourris, but also to make the forerunner of one of today's favorite drinks — ginger ale.

Culture: This is a warm climate crop, not suited to most home gardens here. However, you can grow ginger root in pots indoors in windows, or under lights. Buy really fresh roots — plump, with shiny skins — in specialty shops, and plant just beneath the surface of the soil in slightly moist potting mixture that has lots of sand and some organic humus. When the roots fill the pot, cut away a 3-inch piece to start a new pot, and use the rest for cooking.

If you have too much root for use immediately, freeze it, and cut pieces as needed.

Candied ginger root is made this way:

Candied Ginger

1 lb. fresh ginger root	1 cup cold water
3 cups cold water	1 cup superfine sugar
2 cups granulated sugar	

1. Pare the root and cut into long narrow slices, across the grain. Cover with about 1½ cups cold water in a saucepan and heat to boiling. Simmer 5 minutes, drain, and cover with cold water again. Heat to boiling, simmer 5 minutes more. Drain. Dry well.
2. Combine granulated sugar and 1 cup of water in a small kettle. Boil 10 minutes. Add the ginger slices and cook over very low heat. Do not boil. Stir, and cook until all the syrup is absorbed, about 40 minutes. Remove the ginger, and dry on a rack.
3. Roll the cooled ginger in superfine sugar, and let it stand in the sugar until it has crystalized.

Lavender (*Lavandula,* all species)

Lavender is the herb above all others associated with fragrance in dry perfumes. Both the leaves and the flower buds, picked just before the sprays open on their long, slender stems, have been used for centuries in potpourris, sachets, in moth bags, and as strewing herbs. Distillations have gone into soaps, perfumes, toilet waters, colognes, since these first began to be made in the thirteenth century. One of the early ways of scenting linens was to dry them on the woody lavender shrubs.

Treasured in medieval times, lavender perfumed the silks and chests of the wealthy and was recommended to protect clothes from "all manner of dirty, filthy beasts." It was sprinkled on the heads of maids and young men alike to preserve chastity; and apoplexy, palsy, and loss of speech were only

Lavender

a few of the ills that were said to give way to its "strange, unspeakable virtue." In the fourteenth century Charles VI of France had pillows stuffed with lavender so as always to be surrounded by his favorite scent. In the language of the plants, lavender stood for "silence." One of its most common uses in recent centuries has been as a deterrent to moths, and many old recipes for sachets and sweet bags include both leaves and buds of lavender.

Culture: There are several types of lavender, a woody perennial, cultivated in the modern herb garden. The showiest lavender flowers don't give the most highly scented lavender buds. The best for fragrance is an

English species, *Lavandula spica*. The plant grows to be 3 to 4 feet tall, and spreads about 36 inches across when mature. The fragrant leaves are light gray, rather like pine leaves, and the flowers bloom in late July or August. Some dwarf varieties are offered that are suited to container growing on the patio, terrace, or indoors. 'Hidcote' and 'Munstead Dwarf' are low-growing varieties, about 18 inches tall, offered by many seedsmen. French lavender and Spanish lavender are other species available.

Don't try to grow lavender from seed planted in the open ground. Instead, start seeds indoors in individual peat pots. Place the pots in the refrigerator for 4 weeks, then transfer them to a warm room. Germination should occur in about 14 days. Set the plants outdoors after the weather has warmed and the seedlings are a few inches tall. Lavender grows slowly, which makes it a wonderful plant for low hedges. Its silvery foliage has always made it a favorite for edging knot gardens and formal herb gardens. It is evergreen, and is an especially pretty filler for rose beds.

Soils for lavender should be rich, well drained, and contain lots of organic matter. You can multiply lavender plants by ground layering, and sometimes tip cuttings will root in spring.

A classic lavender potpourri is made as in the recipe below.

Lavender Potpourri

3 cups dried lavender buds	2 Tbs. dried basil
2 Tbs. dried lemon peel	2 Tbs. dried rosemary
4 Tbs. orrisroot powder	1 tsp. benzoic acid powder
4 Tbs. dried spearmint	6 drops oil of lavender

Combine all the ingredients except the oil. Add the oil a drop at a time, tossing as you add. Seal and cure in a dry, airy, warm place for 6 weeks, shaking daily. Pack into a decorative container with a tight stopper.

Lavender Cotton (*Santolina chamaecyparissus*)

Lavender cotton is also commonly called santolina, and sometimes is called French lavender. It is an attractive herb that is grown in gardens for its fragrance and because it is pretty in the landscape. The leaves are used as a moth repellent, and flowering branches are put into winter dried arrangements for their form and continuing fragrance.

Lavender cotton was grown in colonial American gardens, along with woodruff, as a moth repellent, and it was also used as an antiseptic.

Culture: This is an attractive perennial shrub with lots of small branches shaped like coral, bearing grayish leaves. It reaches 12 to 24 inches in height. As a low hedge, or edging for a knot garden, its grayness makes a striking contrast to the other greens of the herbs and flowers. Small, yellow, button-shaped flowers appear in July and August. Use lavender cotton in the rock garden, the herb garden, as a hedge, as a potted plant, or indoors. Santolina comes from the African coast, and is hardy only to about 5° above zero. It does best in rather poor, sandy soil, and in full sunlight. For indoor and container growing, use a mix suited to succulents, with 8 parts sand to 2 parts peat moss, 1 part dried manure, and 1 part vermiculite.

An old-fashioned triple-threat recipe for moth bags includes lavender cotton, rue, and lavender.

French Moth Repellent

3 cups lavender buds	3 cups dried lavender cotton
3 cups dried rue leaves	

Mix well together, and tie into small muslin or cotton bags to place among woolens.

Lemon Balm (*Melissa officinalis*)

Lemon balm leaves, fresh or dried, are used to flavor puddings (use 2 fresh leaves), to

Lemon Balm

make a lemony tea, and are sometimes floated in punch cups and fruit drinks to add a touch of citrus flavor. The primary use of the leaves, however, is in potpourris and sachets. Applied externally, the leaves are still believed by many to have healing powers and to relieve pain. As a cosmetic aid, it is added to skin cleansers. Like bee balm, a perennial whose horticultural name is *Monarda didymus,* lemon balm is credited with attracting bees to a garden, a help when the garden has plants that require cross pollination.

Lemon balm has been called the "long life" herb because the tea made from the leaves was believed to calm nerves and bring sleep. Lemon balm was one of the herbs used to strew floors at weddings in the Middle Ages. Like lavender, it was also used to rub down wooden furniture, leaving behind the sheen of oil and the scent of lemon. "The wine melissa is sodden in is good to keep one from swooning if the cause is colds," *The Grete Herball* reports, and "The leaves tak-

en with salt and eaten will relieve difficulty in breathing and will clear the chest."

Culture: Lemon balm is a perennial that is hardy to about −20°. It reaches about 2 feet at maturity, and makes a broad compact plant that can get weedy looking unless trimmed. The bright green leaves are attractive in a border or on the terrace or patio, where it will grow readily in containers. Buy lemon balm at the garden center, or make root divisions from a friend's garden in spring. Plant lemon balm in sun or semi-sun in soil well supplied with organic matter and fertilizer.

Lemon balm tea is made this way:

Lemon Balm Tea Mixture

2 cups dried lemon balm leaves
1 cup rosebuds
1 cup orange blossoms

Remove leaves from the lemon balm twigs, and discard twigs. Mix leaves with rosebuds and orange blossoms, crushing as you combine. Use 2 teaspoons of this mixture to make 1 cup of tea, and sweeten each cup with 1 teaspoon of honey.

Lemon Verbena (*Lippia citriodorata*)

Lemon verbena is another perennial of the citrus-scented herbs. With lemon balm, the leaves are one of the ingredients often called for in dry perfumes. Steeped in boiling water, they make a refreshing herb tea. The leaves can be used fresh as garnishes for iced punches and as a flavoring agent for puddings and sweets. Lemon verbena leaves are sometimes used in apple and mint jellies.

Lemon verbena doesn't appear to have a long history in European lore. Central and South America are its credited lands of origin, and it is believed to have been brought to Europe, then to North America, by Spanish explorers.

Culture: Lemon verbena is deciduous in cool regions, but evergreen in warm climates. Though it is said to be hardy only to about 10° above zero, I have seen what I thought was lemon verbena growing in climates where temperatures went well below that. At maturity, in mild climates, plants can reach to 10 feet, but in the North, lemon verbena usually stays well under that. Plant lemon verbena as a permanent shrub for scent in mild areas, and grow it as a potted plant on terrace or patio in cooler regions, and bring it indoors for winter. Buy lemon verbena as a young shrub, or root tip cuttings from a friend's plant in spring. Plant in well-drained soil with a good sand content, and enough organic matter to retain moisture during droughts. Set lemon verbena in full sun.

Take leaves as needed for culinary use. Cut back the branches by a third after full summer growth, and dry the leaves for perfumes and tussie-mussies.

Two old-fashioned ways in which lemon verbena was used — as a flavoring for jelly, and as an herbal bath—follow.

Apple Jelly with Lemon Verbena Leaves

| 12 acid cooking apples (about 4 lbs.) | 8 cups sugar |
| 1 cup water | 10 lemon verbena leaves |

1. Chop the cored apples, and in a heavy enamel kettle, simmer them with the water until soft, about 25 minutes. Place the apples and juices in a jelly bag to drain overnight; set a glass bowl under the bag to catch the draining apple juice. It should make 10 cups.
2. The next day, set the apple juice and the sugar to simmer in a large jam or jelly kettle. Heat to boiling, then simmer until the juice flowing from a metal spoon sheets rather than falls in drops. Put 1 lemon verbena leaf into each of 10 sterilized 8-ounce jelly glasses, and pour the jelly over them. Seal with paraffin, and cap. Keep stored in a cool room.

Herbal Bath with Lemon Verbena

Pick 4 leafy tips from lemon verbena plants, tie them into a cheesecloth bag, and boil in 2 cups of water for 15 minutes. Discard the herb, and pour the water into a drawn bath.

Marjoram (*Marjorana hortensis*)

There is some confusion about marjorams: The species called sweet marjoram is *Majorana hortensis,* an herb used in flavoring foods and also in scenting potpourris and sachets. However, marjoram is also the common name for *Origanum,* which is also called oregano. *Origanum* is also referred to as pot marjoram and as wild marjoram. The way I distinguish between the two plants is to call *Majorana hortensis* sweet marjoram, and to

Marjoram

call *Origanum* pot marjoram, unless I call it oregano. Which is which doesn't matter too much to the average user, except that you should know that sweet marjoram is an annual and has a milder flavor, while pot marjoram, or oregano, has a strong flavor, and is a perennial.

Use the leaves of sweet marjoram, fresh or dried, with lamb, pork, beef, veal, chicken, fish. Crumble the leaves over the meats before cooking them, then remove them before serving. Sweet marjoram is also excellent with tomato dishes, broccoli, on pizza, in spaghetti sauce, in egg dishes. Sweet marjoram vinegar adds flavor to salads and marinades. Use the dried leaves in potpourris and sachets.

Sweet marjoram is a native of Western Asia and the Mediterranean. It figures in herbal lore as one of the strewing herbs, and the Greeks believed that sweet marjoram found growing wild on a grave meant that the departed was contented and at peace. Bridal wreaths were made from branches of sweet marjoram.

Culture: A perennial in very mild climates, sweet marjoram is nearly always grown as an annual in this country. It has attractive velvety leaves and tiny white blossoms that appear in summer. It can be grown in the open garden, or in containers or window boxes, but it is prettiest if it is kept trimmed to under 12 inches. Pot up sweet marjoram at the end of the summer and bring it indoors to a sunny windowsill or a light garden. Plant sweet marjoram seed in early spring in individual peat pots, and transplant pot and all outdoors when the weather warms. Germination takes about 10 to 15 days. Set sweet marjoram in full sun, in well-drained soil on the sweet side. Keep watered during dry spells.

Sweet marjoram is excellent with lamb or veal in herb mixtures like the one below. Its use with fruit is illustrated in the recipe for Applesauce and Raisin Relish.

Herb Mixture with Marjoram for Lamb or Veal

1 tsp. dried sweet
  marjoram

1 tsp. dried rosemary

1 tsp. dried summer savory

1 tsp. dried parsley

1 tsp. dried chervil

Crush all the herbs together, mix well, and bottle. Sprinkle 1 teaspoon over lamb or veal before cooking.

Applesauce and Raisin Relish

1 cup applesauce
½ cup seedless
  raisins

2 Tbs. grated
  orange rind
½ tsp. dried sweet
  marjoram

Combine applesauce with raisins that have been soaked for 5 minutes in hot water, then drained. Add orange peel and crushed marjoram. Chill 2 hours before serving.

Mint (*Mentha,* all species)

The mints are a large group of perennial herbs used for flavoring foods and for scenting bath bags, potpourris, and moth bags. The species most important in flavoring is

Mint

Mentha spicata, spearmint. This is the one to grow for flavoring jellies and confections, and is the type often used to make chewing gum. It makes a delightful tea, and adds flavor to Indian and Greek dishes, to lamb, to cooked fresh green peas, and to carrots. Orange mint, which is also called bergamot mint (*Mentha citrata*), is also grown to flavor potpourris, as is peppermint. Golden apple mint (*Mentha gentilis*) and apple mint are sometimes used in jellies. Pineapple mint and apple mint are probably the most desirable from an aesthetic point of view, but less useful for culinary purposes and potpourris than spearmint.

Spearmint is from the Mediterranean area and was known in ancient times as a symbol of hospitality. In France it was called Our Lady's mint, and in Italy, *Erba Santa Maria.* In the tussie-mussie, it stands for wisdom. In the Middle Ages it was crushed and rubbed on table tops, and strewn in bedrooms and banquet halls to scent the air, crushed as a perfume for the bath, and rubbed on the teeth to sweeten the breath. Peppermint became known in the seventeenth century when it was found growing wild in England. Medicinally, mint was used as a toothache remedy, to stop vomiting, and to kill internal parasites. Pennyroyal (*Mentha pulegium*) was a remedy for sickness at sea, for head colds, for congestion.

Culture: Mints are perennials that grow easily — too easily — and spread by underground runners. If you aren't careful, they'll take over the whole garden. To confine mints, plant them as root divisions in large bottomless cans sunk into the soil. That allows the roots to go down, but not out too freely. Hardy to about −20°, mints are most successful in semi-shade and in soil well supplied with organic humus. You can grow plants from cuttings taken from a friend's mint plants and rooted in water in early spring. They grow to 18 to 24 inches tall.

Here are a few of the ways in which mints are used.

Fresh Mint Leaf Sauce for Lamb

3 Tbs. cold water	1½ tsp. confectioners sugar
⅓ cup mint leaves, finely chopped	⅓ cup strong vinegar

In a small saucepan, combine the water and the sugar and, over low heat, stir until the sugar dissolves. Add mint leaves and vinegar, mix well, and allow to marinate 30 minutes before serving.

Dried Mint Leaf Tea

4 Tbs. dried spearmint leaves	½ Tbs. sugar or 1 Tbs. honey
4 8-oz. cups boiling water	

Scald a large teapot, and place the leaves in it. Bring the water to a rapid boil and pour at once over the leaves. Allow to steep for 5 minutes. Add sweetening, stir up once, then pour through a strainer. Makes 4 cups.

Apple, Mint Leaf, and Orange Relish

1 unpeeled orange	½ cup fresh mint leaves, chopped
1 cup applesauce	

Grate the orange rind, chop the orange pulp, and combine with applesauce and the mint leaves. Stir well, and marinate for several hours before serving.

Moneywort (*Lysimachia nummularia*)

Moneywort is an herb used in fragrance and is an effective moth repellent. In modern gardens it is grown primarily as a ground cover.

Culture: Moneywort (and it is also called loosestrife, and creeping jennie) is a perennial you can buy by the seed packet or as started plants. It is hardy to about −20°. An attractive form is *Lysimachia nummularia aurea,* or golden moneywort. Only 1 to 2 inches tall at maturity, it is planted to create a rapid ground cover or where a golden accent is needed. It is a creeping trailer whose leaves are a true golden yellow. The plant bears showy yellow flowers on short stems through June, July, and August. The flowers are fragrant and should be picked just before full bloom for drying. The plant can be used

Moneywort

Cape Cod Moth Repellent

6 cups dried
  moneywort
6 cups dried tansy

6 cups dried laven-
  der cotton

Crush the dried herbs together, mix well, and place in muslin bags. Tie with ribbons and set among the woolens.

Nasturtium (*Tropaeolum, all species*)

The nasturtium, a charming, old-fashioned flower that grows easily everywhere, is enormously decorative, and has many uses as a flavoring herb. Nasturtium leaves, and its edible, gloriously bright orange-through-gold flowers, have a peppery flavor reminiscent of watercress, and are excellent in salads. The flowers add a tangy flavor and color to sandwiches with cream cheese, and can be used to decorate any dish where a strong peppery flavor is suitable. After the flowers have gone, the plants ripen little round seeds that look like capers. They can be pickled in vinegar, and used as home-grown capers, or sprinkled fresh through salads, and in thick, starchy soups. The flowers, dried, make a colorful addition to potpourris. Pull flowers that have just fully opened apart to dry.

In the tussie-mussie, nasturtiums stand for patriotism.

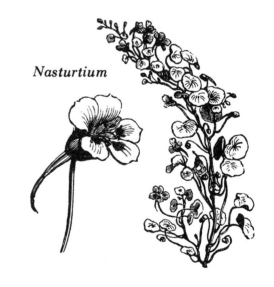

Nasturtium

as an edging, in the rock garden, or in hanging baskets or container gardens. Plant it in full sun, or semi-sun, in soil well supplied with organic humus that will hold moisture. Or plant in a moist area where the soil has enough sand for good drainage. Set the plants 3 to 10 inches apart for ground cover. Divide the third year.

A typical herbal moth repellent combines moneywort and lavender cotton with tansy.

Culture: Nasturtiums are perennial flowers in Central and South America, their lands of origin, but in all except the warm areas of this country, they are grown as annuals. In herb gardens, the most popular species is *Trapaeolum majus,* which trails or climbs around an upright support, and a small type, offered by Burpee Seeds as 'Double Dwarf Jewel,' which grows to about 12 inches tall. The nasturtiums are easy to grow and bloom lavishly even in the most ordinary soil, as long as it is well drained. They will bloom in dry seashore locations and even in gravel areas. Don't fertilize soil for nasturtiums, or you'll get more leaves than flowers. Sow seeds where the plants are to bloom, or start them indoors in individual peat pots a few weeks before the soil warms. Seeds take 7 to 10 days to germinate. Nasturtiums grow rapidly, and will come into bloom a few weeks after sowing. Use trailing kinds to cover fences, or banks, to drip down walls, or in containers, or baskets. Use the dwarfs as bedding plants, and to cover fading spring bulbs. At the end of the season, bring the youngest plants indoors and try them on a sunny windowsill. They'll continue to bloom for some time.

Here are recipes showing how nasturtiums can be used in salads, and to make capers.

Nasturtium Salad

2 cups iceberg lettuce, torn	4 fresh nasturtium seeds
2 cups oakleaf lettuce, torn	8 fresh nasturtium flowers
4 nasturtium leaves, torn	¼ cup French dressing

In a serving bowl, set the lettuces, the nasturtium leaves, the seeds and the flowers. Chill. Just before serving, toss all with the dressing.

Nasturtium Seed Capers

2 cups fresh nasturtium seeds	¼ cup salt
1 cup water	1 cup sugar
	1 cup malt vinegar

Wash the seeds, dry them, and set in a small crock. Mix the water and the salt, and pour over the seeds. Cover, and let stand at room temperature for 2 days. Drain the water, and pour the seeds into a small, sterile jar. Heat sugar and vinegar to boiling, pour over the seeds, seal. Let set 4 weeks before using.

Oregano (*Origanum vulgare*)

Oregano is also called pot marjoram and wild marjoram. It is a cooking herb with a flavor similar to, but stronger than, sweet marjoram. The flavor resembles thyme, and the dried leaves can be used as a substitute for thyme in potpourri and sachet recipes. Use the leaves, fresh or dried, in Italian, Spanish, and Mexican cuisine, and in Greek and Turkish cooking. It is sometimes called the pizza herb since its distinctive flavor is one you always find in a well-made pizza. One teaspoon of fresh, or ½ teaspoon of dried, oregano is all you should begin any seasoning adventure with. Crumble dried leaves, and mince fresh leaves, before using. Spaghetti sauces, zucchini dishes, tomato salads, and cooked tomato dishes are all good with oregano added. Sprinkle the minced

Oregano

fresh herb over green salads before serving. Chili con carne, barbeque sauces, vegetable soups with tomatoes, onion dishes, pork, lamb, fish, and chicken are all improved with a dash of oregano.

The Greeks wove legends around oregano, and called it "joy of the mountain." It was a must in every medieval garden, and was used before hops were discovered in the making of ale and to flavor elaborately spiced wines. In early American cookbooks it is referred to as wild marjoram. It is only since World War II, when American soldiers discovered Italy and things Italian, that the name oregano came to be used.

Culture: Oregano is a perennial, hardy to about −25°. It reaches 24 to 30 inches at maturity, and is a shrubby plant. Started from seed, cuttings, or root divisions in spring, and planted in full sun in ordinary garden soil with sand and humus added, oregano will grow rapidly, and if you aren't careful, it will spread well beyond your intentions. Clip it to keep it attractive and in bounds, and to collect herbs for drying. Oregano can be continually clipped to form a low hedge for the herb garden. Unclipped, it will produce small purple and pink florets in August. It is a good subject for a hot, dry, rock garden, or to top a rock wall. Pot up sturdy young plants in fall and bring them indoors to a sunny windowsill to provide you with fresh oregano all winter.

The use of oregano in pizzas can be seen in this quick pizza made with English muffins.

Quick Pizza Sandwiches with Oregano

4 English muffins	4 mushrooms
¼ cup chili sauce	2 tsp. dried oregano
¼ cup Mozzarella, grated	2 Tbs. olive oil
2 hot dogs, or 4 slices garlic or Italian sausage	

1. Slice the muffins into halves, or tear them into halves with two forks. Under a medium broiler, toast the smooth side until quite brown and dry.
2. Remove the muffins from the oven, turn them over, and spread them with chili sauce, sprinkle with cheese, add hot dog or sausage slices. Cut each mushroom in 3 pieces, and divide over the pieces of muffins. Sprinkle ¼ teaspoon oregano over each slice, and drizzle each slice with olive oil. Broil under a medium broiler until the cheese bubbles and is melted. Serve at once.

Parsley (*Petroselinum crispum*)

Parsley is probably the one herb a cook couldn't do without — at least not a French cook. A flavoring herb — though it occasionally has been used as a strewing herb — it is used fresh in innumerable recipes for stocks, soups, stews, casseroles, omelets, sauces. Minced, fresh leaves are added to all sorts of salads and vegetable dishes, hors d'oeuvres, and are spread as bright green garnishes for canapes and decorated platters. Use ½ cup of very finely minced fresh parsley to garnish beef stews and kidney dishes, or any strongly

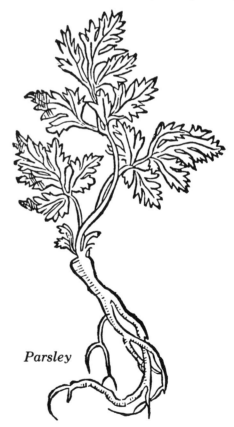

Parsley

flavored game casserole. Cover sliced tomatoes with finely minced parsley, drizzle with French dressing, and flavor with crushed garlic. Butter tiny boiled new potatoes and toss them in minced parsley and coarse salt to taste. Dress baked fish with parsley minced with chives and fresh mushrooms, and dot with butter 5 minutes before the dish finishes cooking. Sprinkle minced parsley into scrambled eggs or over canned hot soups. Use sprigs of parsley as a garnish for any vegetable or meat dish. Chew a handful to sweeten your breath — it works.

Parsley comes to us from the shores of the Mediterranean where it has been used as a cooking herb for thousands of years. A fable explains its origin: Juno's horses cropped parsley in Elysian pastures to make them spirited. At Greek banquets, parsley crowns were offered to guests to improve their appetites and serenity. In the language of the plants, parsley stands for rejoicing. *Banckes's* (sic) *Herbal* said of parsley, "It multiplieth greatly a man's blood."

Culture: Parsley is a biennial, and grows almost anywhere in moderately rich, well-drained soil that has some organic humus to retain moisture. It grows almost as well in shade as it does in full sun. It will grow in pots, in container gardens, in window boxes, in the open garden, and makes an attractive edging plant anywhere. In the fall, pot it up — dig deep to get all of the tap root — cut the stems back by a third, and bring it indoors to a sunny windowsill. Or grow it under fluorescent lights indoors. Sow parsley seeds, or set out as purchased potted plants. The seeds germinate in about 10 to 15 days indoors, but outdoors not for about 3 weeks. Soak them overnight in warm water before planting. Keep the soil moist and warm until the seeds germinate. Because it's a biennial, parsley will grow up again the second year, but will quickly go to seed. Keep the flower heads picked as they appear this second season, and plant fresh parsley seed near the old bed. By the time last year's plants are too played out and bitter for use, the new plants will be ready for picking. Pick sprigs at will, but never strip a plant completely. Cut the plants back by half in midsummer, and freeze or dry parsley for winter use.

Parsley Salad

6 Tbs. olive oil	1/8 tsp. black pepper
1 1/2 Tbs. vinegar	1 large head ice-
1/4 tsp. dry mustard	berg lettuce, torn
1/4 tsp. granulated	1/2 cup finely minced
sugar	parsley
1/8 tsp. salt	

Mix all the ingredients but the lettuce and the parsley in the blender at low speed for 1 minute. Chill them, and then chill the lettuce. Just before serving, toss the lettuce with the dressing, then with the parsley.

Peppers, Sweet and Hot (*Capsicum annuum*)

The common garden peppers, both sweet types and hot types, are varieties of *Capsicum annuum*. This is a distinctly different plant from the one that produces the black or white pepper that belongs on the spice shelf, *Piper nigrum*, a tropical vine. The sweet and the hot peppers are suitable for the herb garden, and are pretty enough to grow in containers or in the flower border. Plant hot peppers in quantity only if you plan to use lots for pickling, or if you do a lot of Mexican cooking. Use the sweet peppers fresh in salads, in Italian dishes with veal, in *ratatouille,* or stuff them with rice or meat mixtures.

South America is the place of origin of the capsicum family. When Columbus arrived, a member of his party reported that there were innumerable kinds of *Ages,* the Indian name for pod peppers, some red, some yellow, some violet, some brown, some white, and all shapes and sizes.

Culture: Start sweet peppers from seed indoors several weeks before the air will warm to 70° outdoors, or buy started plants from the garden center. After the weather is holding at a steady 70°, set the seedlings in good garden loam with lots of organic matter added, 2 feet apart in rows 3 feet apart. Keep well watered until they begin to grow, and

Sweet Pepper

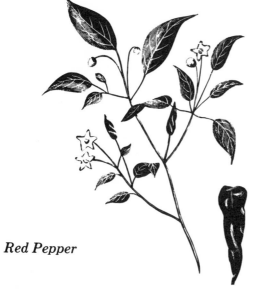

Red Pepper

Peppers aren't dried as are other herbs. The two sets of instructions below tell what to do with each kind — the sweet and the hot —of pepper.

Drying Hot Peppers

Pick the peppers when ripe. Wear gloves. Spread the peppers one layer deep on screens and set the screens in sunlight during the hottest part of the day. Bring them indoors to keep them from nighttime humidity. When they are crackling dry, seal into large canning jars, and store.

Freezing Sweet Peppers

Wash freshly picked, full-grown peppers, cut out the stems and the cores, and remove the seeds. Scrape out as much white pulp as possible. Slice into rounds, or into wedges, and seal into heavy-duty freezer bags. Set to freeze in a flash-freezing unit, or on the freezing coils in the freezer. Remove the rings as needed for cooking and reseal the bag.

Stuffed Peppers

8 large sweet peppers	Salt and pepper to taste
2 Tbs. olive oil	1 small bay leaf
2 onions, peeled and slivered	¼ tsp. thyme
¾ lb. ground lamb	2 cups cooked rice
2 tomatoes, peeled and chopped	1 cup tomato sauce
1 clove garlic, peeled and minced	2 Tbs. butter
	2 tsp. fresh basil, minced

1. Preheat over to 350°.
2. Wash, core, and seed the peppers, and cut off the tops. Boil the peppers and tops rapidly in water to cover, for 5 minutes. Drain well.
3. In a large skillet, heat the oil and sauté the onions until lightly browned. Add the meat and brown, stirring constantly. Stir in the tomatoes, garlic, salt and pepper to taste, bay leaf, and thyme. Cook until the tomatoes are pulpy, but not dry. Add the cooked rice, and mix well. Remove from the heat.

when they begin to mature fruit. Keep the peppers picked as they reach maturity to encourage the plant to mature more. If your sweet peppers still have lots of fruit when frosts threaten, cover with big brown paper bags or old sheets to see them through this first cold wave, and they will continue to ripen fruit as long as the good weather holds. The edible hot peppers (not the popular houseplant of the same name) grow well as potted plants indoors, and will even ripen fruit.

4. Stuff the peppers with the rice mixture, and replace the caps. Place in an oiled baking dish, and bake 10 to 20 minutes — 20 if the peppers are very thick. During the last few minutes of cooking time, heat the tomato sauce, melt the butter into it, season with fresh basil, and pour over the peppers before serving.
Serves 6 to 8.

Hot Mexican Chili with Peppers

¼ cup vegetable oil	1 lb. ground beef
¾ cup chopped onions	6 hot peppers
½ cup chopped sweet peppers	2 cups tomato sauce
2 cloves garlic, peeled and minced	2 tsp. minced fresh oregano, or 1 tsp. dried
2 cups cooked kidney beans	Salt to taste

1. Heat the oil in a heavy kettle, and sauté the onions, sweet peppers, and garlic, until the onions are transparent, about 5 minutes.
2. Stir in the kidney beans, and simmer while you seed and chop the hot peppers. Add the ground meat, chili peppers, tomato sauce, oregano, and salt to taste. Mash the beans into the liquid to thicken it. When the meat is cooked, turn off the heat and let the dish stand for an hour before serving.
Serves 6

Rose (*Rosa,* all species)

An herb garden for fragrance must have roses. Rose petals are the backbone of the moist potpourri, and of dry potpourris and sachets as well. Rose petals are edible, and historically were used for flavoring as well as for scent. Candied rose petals and rose buds make delightful garnishes for gala desserts.

Always a primary source of fragrance, roses have figured in romantic stories from the days of early Egypt through the heyday of the Greeks, the Roman Empire, and into the Renaissance. Cleopatra strewed rose petals knee-deep when receiving Mark Antony. Petals of fragrant roses filled the halls during Roman and Greek banquets, and were strewn in the streets during triumphant marches. In Greek mythology, roses were believed to have sprung from the blood of Aphrodite, the goddess of love, and Adonis, the handsome lover, who was killed by a wild boar. Marie Antoinette is just one of a long list of romantic heroines who surrounded herself with the scent of roses. In the language of the plants, red roses stand for love, white for silence, and yellow roses are an accusation of lack of fidelity. To the people of the Middle Ages, the rose was the "flower of flowers," a remedy for everything from heartache to skin blemishes. A syrup of honey and roses was given to "feeble, sick, phlegmatic, melancholy, and chloric people."

Culture: When potpourris were made long ago, they depended mainly on the fragrance

Rose

of roses for their scent. Roses then were less showy, and more perfumed. Old-fashioned fragrant flowers that you can find at some nurseries today are the Damask roses, 'Agnes,' which is yellow; 'Celsiana,' a pink; 'Jacques Cartier,' another pink; 'Rose de Rescht,' a fuschia red; 'Rose du Roi,' a red. The rugosa roses 'Hansa,' 'Belle Poitevine,' and 'Frau Dagmar Hastrup,' along with the Common Moss Cabbage rose, and the Crested Moss Cabbage rose, and two hybrid perpetuals, 'General Jacqueminot' and 'Reine des Violettes,' are other old-fashioned fragrant roses.

Among fragrant roses of today are the hybrid teas such as 'Candy Stripe,' 'Crimson Glory,' 'Étoile de Holland,' 'Mirandy,' 'Mr. Lincoln,' 'Fragrant Cloud,' 'Helen Traubel,' 'Talisman,' 'The Doctor,' and 'Tiffany.' There are others, and will be more. Big breeders, such as Jackson and Perkins, have been concentrating in recent years on bringing fragrance to some of the best roses, and are working on old favorites that had exceptional fragrance.

Among dealers interested in old fragrant roses are Joseph J. Kern Rose Nursery, Box 33, Mentor, Ohio 44060; Tillotson's Roses, 802 Brown's Valley Road, Watsonville, California 95076; and Melvin E. Wyant, Johnny Cake Ridge, Mentor, Ohio 44060.

In selecting roses for use in dry perfumes, remember that the very dark colors tend to dry to a murky shade, and that the pastels, in particular the pinks, are best in potpourris. Plant roses in full sunlight. They grow either in the open garden or in containers on terrace or patio. They are not good houseplants in varieties suited to the making of dry perfumes. In hot areas, avoid planting roses near a wall which will reflect excessive heat in summer. The soil should be well supplied with humus, and really fertile. Add a liberal amount of bone meal to the planting hole; it is a slow-release fertilizer that will continue to feed the plants in the years to come. Fertilize every spring with an all-purpose, or a rose, fertilizer before the plants start to leaf out. If black spot or beetles are problems in your area, follow a spray pro-

gram. Rose spray containers describe them. Prune rose branches back in fall, mound in cold areas after the ground has frozen, and cut the branches back again in spring to remove any dead wood at their tips.

The recipe below is typical of the use of rose petals in a dry potpourri.

Rose Bowl

4 cups bone-dry rose petals	2 Tbs. ground all-spice
2 cups dried rose leaves	¼ cup ground cloves
2 Tbs. ground cinnamon	2 ground tonka beans
3 cups dried lavender buds	6 drops oil of roses
⅓ cup orrisroot powder	3 drops oil of lavender

Combine all the dry ingredients, mix well, and add the oils, a drop at a time, mixing as you work. Seal into a jar, and cure for 6 weeks in a dry, dark, warm place that is well ventilated. Shake the jar daily. When cured, turn the potpourri into a decorative container with a tightly stoppered lid. Open only when the potpourri is in use.

Rosemary (*Rosmarinus officinalis*)

Rosemary is one of the most attractive plants to the herb gardener, because it is useful as a fragrance herb, and because it is useful as a flavoring herb, and because it looks well in the herb garden and in the flower border, or most anywhere else. One-half teaspoon of rosemary, dried or fresh, crushed and added to roasting lamb, poultry, veal, beef, pork, baked fish, stews, to soups, and marinades changes the whole flavor scale. You can use it in Italian and Spanish and Latin American meat and pasta sauces. Use the minced leaves fresh in salads and with green beans, eggplant dishes, summer squash, mushroom sauces, and soups. Add 1 teaspoon dried to the fat for deep frying, or to the water for boiling rice. Try it with spoon breads, with shrimp dishes, and mayonnaise

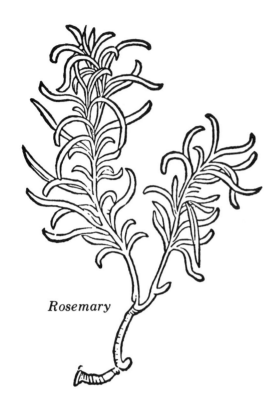

Rosemary

were painted on a heart and sent as a token of affection on St. Valentine's Day. In England, gilded branches of rosemary were given to wedding guests, and it was an important item in tussie-mussies for weddings. Shakespeare referred to it in Hamlet, when Ophelia puts together a tussie-mussie for Hamlet after he has killed her father. The first line reads, "There's rosemary, that's for remembrance."

Culture: Rosemary grows well in sandy, even poor, soil as long as the soil is sweet — on the alkaline side. And it needs sun. A perennial, it is hardy only to about 0°. Rosemary can be trained to tree forms in pots, too. The plants get to be about 2 feet tall in cooler climates, but sometimes climb to 6 feet in warm regions, where it often is used as edging material. Plant seeds indoors, as they are slow to germinate. Or root tip cuttings in spring and transplant to the outdoors when the weather warms. Plant in the open garden, in ornamental borders, in large containers on the terrace, or grow rosemary as a pot plant for transfer to the indoors when the weather cools. The variety 'Prostratus' is a low-growing type that makes a good ground cover. The leaves of rosemary are glossy green on the top side, and grayish underneath, and they look like pine needles. Flowers are lavender or blue and cover the foliage in summer.

The simple moth repellent below combines rosemary and lavender. The recipe for rubbing lotion can be used with thyme, lavender, verbena, mint, and marjoram as well as rosemary. The herb pillow makes a welcome gift.

as dip for cold cocktail shrimp. Bake turnips in butter and rosemary sealed in heavy-duty foil. And try a little crushed rosemary with a citrus fruit salad. As a fragrance herb, rosemary is used in moth bags, and in potpourris with lemon verbena. It makes a sweet sleeping pillow, a sachet for linens, and is marvelous with wormwood and lavender and mint.

Rosemary has a long history. It has been a symbol of fidelity in lovers for more than 2,000 years, and in medieval times, was sometimes burned as incense in religious ceremonies. One of the most loved and useful medicinal herbs, it was also used in salads, fish sauces, and as a flavoring for wine. Garlands of rosemary decorated the boar's head at Christmas and rosemary-scented water was offered to guests for washing after meals. It was considered a powerful charm against the "evil eye." In colonial America, it was used as a strewing herb, along with thyme and woodruff. In wedding bouquets, it was a symbol of remembrance. Sprigs of rosemary

Moth Repellent with Rosemary

2 cups dried lavender	1 Tbs. crushed cloves
2 cups dried rosemary	Dried peel of a lemon

Bruise all the ingredients together in a small bowl, and divide among muslin bags. Tie, and set among the woolens.

Rubbing Lotion with Rosemary

1 cup of rosemary leaves	1 quart rubbing alcohol

Crush the leaves in the bottom of a 1-quart glass jar, and pour the alcohol over the leaves. Cap tightly, and let stand 2 weeks. Strain through cheesecloth, rebottle, cap tightly. Use after the bath.

Herb Pillow with Rosemary

4 cups dried rosemary	8 cups dry pine needles
4 cups dried lemon verbena	

Crush the ingredients together, and fill a small bag to place under the pillow, or in the drawer with nightclothes.

Rue (*Ruta graveolens*)

Rue, an attractive evergreen shrub with unusual flowers, is grown primarily as a fragrance herb, but does have culinary uses. It is one of the herbs that flavors aromatic vinegars, and is added sparingly to Italian salads. The leaves and the seed heads are appealing in tussie-mussies and other dried arrangements. In country homes in Europe, it is put into beds to discourage bugs, and hung in the kitchen to keep flies away.

It has a long history as a disinfectant. During plague epidemics, rue and pitch were burned in the streets. In the seventeenth century, herbal vinegars were made to ward off bad odors and the diseases people believed they carried, and rue figured prominently in most of these recipes. Eventually, these aromatic vinegars went into little containers called "vinaigrettes," which ladies wore on chains and sniffed when fainting seemed a probability. Rue also was used to deter pests, and was so trusted in France as a safeguard against moths that it is one of the herbs called *garderobe,* literally, "guardian of robes." The forerunner of the tussie-mussie probably was the little bunch of rue carried

Rue

as a preventive against plagues. In time, these dried nosegays came to include herbs and dried flowers and developed more romantic connotations. In the language of the plants, rue stands for repentance and grief. Bunches of dried rue were hung to fend off witches.

Culture: Rue is a perennial, hardy to about −20°. It reaches 24 to 36 inches grown outdoors, but stays smaller when grown as a pot plant indoors. You can start rue from seed, or buy root divisions. Start seed indoors and set out after the weather warms. Plant rue in full sun, in a rather sweet soil with lots of organic matter and a liberal dose of general fertilizer. Prune potted rue persistently to keep the form compact. Indoors grow it in your sunniest window, or under lights. Fertilize once a month with a balanced fertilizer.

The recipe below is an adaptation of the vinegar recipes of the Middle Ages. The scent is sharp and spicy.

Rue Vinegar for the Bath

1 cup tightly packed fresh rue leaves	2 slices fresh ginger root, or 1 tsp. ginger powder
1 cup tightly packed fresh sage leaves	2 cups white vinegar
	2 cups water

In a small saucepan, bring the water and the vinegar to a rapid boil, and throw in the herbs and the ginger. Allow to boil up once, then remove from the heat and steep overnight. Strain, then bottle. Use 1 cupful for a tub of bath water.

Sage (*Salvia,* all species)

Sage was thought of once primarily as a medicinal herb, but today it is used more for flavoring and scenting than for curing. Sage is the dominant flavoring in stuffings for poultry, including the Thanksgiving turkey, and for fish and pork. Use the leaves, fresh or dried, crumbled over roasts, in soups, sauces, chowders, marinades, lima bean dishes, onion dishes, with eggplant, tomato, cheese, and potatoes. Try it in your favorite meat loaf recipe, and blend a dash of ground, dried sage into cheese spreads.

In the Middle Ages, sage was well toward the top of the list of important herbs. It was taken to help the memory, and thought to improve longevity. Tussie-mussies of sage and chamomile were given to wish a friend sagacity, long life, and patience. Its sharp scent was considered a protection against all sorts of illness, and along with rue, it was an ingredient in vinegars made as preventatives against plagues, and to clean the air in the sick room. As a culinary herb, it was used in pork dishes, and as a scent herb it was used to make water for washing hands after meals.

Culture: There are many types of sage on the market. The salvias used ornamentally have brilliant spikes of red or blue flowers, but these are not the types used for flavoring. The cooking herb is *Salvia officinalis,* a perennial. 'Mammoth Sage,' a variety, is preferred. It has gray-green leaves which stay on the plant all year. In the cold North, *Salvia officinalis* grows as a sprawling silvery shrubby affair with somewhat woody stems, and it creeps all over the garden, tends to lie down on the job and generally loses its lower leaves, which makes it knobby-kneed. In milder areas, it grows as a fragrant ground cover suited to rocky areas and slopes. Sage can be grown outdoors, or in as a potted plant as well. Pineapple sage, *Salvia rutilans,* has leaves that really do smell of pineapple when rubbed or crumbled. This is a 2- to 3-foot perennial that bears scarlet flowers late in the season when grown outdoors. It's

Sage

an attractive plant for the indoor garden as well. Clary sage, *Salvia Sclarea,* is a biennial with whitish flowers that have a strong aromatic odor. The leaves of this type are used for flavoring, and the seeds are used commercially in perfume-making.

Sow sage seeds indoors in March. Germination takes about 14 days. Or sow outdoors in late spring. Germination outdoors takes 21 to 30 days, so be patient. You can also grow sage from cuttings taken in spring, and it can be ground layered. Plant sage, which is hardy to about −30°, in a sunny spot, in soil on the dry side, but rich in organic humus and fertilizer.

Typical stuffing using sage is made from the recipe below.

Sage Stuffing for Pork or Fish

2 Tbs. butter	1 tsp. dried, ground
¾ cup onion,	sage
minced	¼ cup parsley,
2 cups bread	minced
crumbs	⅛ tsp. allspice
¼ cup beef bouillon	½ tsp. salt
1 clove garlic,	⅛ tsp. pepper
peeled and	1 egg
mashed	

1. In a medium saucepan, melt the butter and simmer the onions until translucent. Remove from the heat.
2. In a mixing bowl, combine onion and pan juices with the remaining ingredients and mix well. Spread the stuffing along the cut between the pork ribs and the back bone. Tie the roast firmly with white string, and bake ½ hour longer than for unstuffed pork.

Savory (*Satureja,* all species)

There are two types of savory: summer savory, a shrubby annual, is *Satureja hortensis,* the herb intended in most recipes calling for savory; winter savory, *Satureja montana,* is an evergreen woody speecies with a much stronger flavor. Some cooks claim that a few leaves of winter savory cooked along with

Savory

lima, black, or lentil beans not only does wonders for the flavor but also eliminates the gaseous effects of these foods. Sprinkle summer, or winter, savory on green beans, meats of all kinds, chicken, in dressings, scrambled eggs, and omelets during cooking. Use 1 teaspoon fresh, or ½ teaspoon dried, summer savory, and a little less of the winter type. Crumble a few savory leaves over fried chicken 10 minutes before the end of the cooking. It's a great change. Use the fresh crushed leaves of summer savory on bee stings — it is said to take away the pain.

In medieval times, savory was added to food when a peppery accent was wanted, but it was "forbidden to use it much in meats" according to *Banckes's* (sic) *Herbal,* since it "stirreth him that useth lechery." It was recommended as a purgative, to correct liver and lung problems, and as a bleach for tanned skin.

Culture: The annual, or summer, savory can be grown from seed sown in the open garden in spring (May) where the plants are to stay. Seeds germinate in about 7 days. Sow thickly, and thin the plants to stand 4 to 6 inches apart. Summer savory prefers a soil lightened with peat moss and rich in organic matter. Plant summer and winter savories in full sun. Winter savory, the perennial type, makes an excellent houseplant if cut back frequently. It is evergreen, rather woody, grows to about 15 inches tall, and has stiff, narrow, shiny leaves. The tiny white flowers, sometimes pink or purplish in cast, are long-lasting, and outdoors, they attract bees. Winter savory makes a decorative plant for border edgings and is often used to create a low hedge. It is hardy to about −20°. Seeds of this type are very slow to germinate, so buy started plants, or take divisions from a friend's plants, or root cuttings in early spring. Winter savory prefers sandy, well-drained soil, and requires less moisture than the summer savory.

The recipes below suggest herbs that blend well with the savories.

Herb Mixture for Beef Dishes

3 Tbs. dried summer savory, or 2 Tbs. winter savory	3 Tbs. sweet marjoram
3 Tbs. dried sweet basil	3 Tbs. dried parsley
	3 Tbs. dried chervil

Crush all the leaves together in a large bowl, mix well, and bottle tightly. Use 1 teaspoon of the mixed herbs as flavoring.

Herb Mixture for Pork Dishes

3 Tbs. dried summer savory, or 2 Tbs. winter savory	3 Tbs. dried sage
	3 Tbs. dried rosemary
3 Tbs. dried sweet basil	

Crush all the leaves together in a large bowl, mix well, and bottle tightly. Use 1 teaspoon of the mixed herbs as flavoring.

Shallots (*Allium ascalonicum*)

The shallot tastes like a cross between an onion and a garlic clove. It is encased in an orangey skin and grows as two or more cloves grouped together in a manner similar to that of a head of garlic. Much sought after by devotees of French cuisine, shallots are often hard to find. The flavor is used much in cooking fish, to make gourmet butters to dress boiled begetables, and without shallots you can't make a proper butter for baked snails. (Which may or may not appeal to you.)

Culture: Seedsmen and catalogs sell shallots for planting, and those offered by specialty food markets are suited to planting, too. Break the head apart, separate and plant the cloves, broad end down, in soil that has been well fertilized, and made light with the addition of organic humus. Plant shallots when the frost is out of the ground in holes 1 inch deep, and about 6 inches apart. Cover with ½ inch soil, and tamp firmly. Shallots grow tall, tuberous stems, like those of chives but larger, which eventually bear a round seed head. Bend all the stems when a few have fallen over of themselves to help the plant to mature the onion-like bulb. Dig these on a sunny day, leave in the garden for 2 or 3 days to cure in the sun, then braid the shallots by their stems, and hang in a cool, dry, dark place for winter use.

The two butters made with shallots here are typical of gourmet uses of this wonderful herb. Use the Shallot Butter to finish fish or steaks. Stuff snails with the Butter for Snails after you have inserted the canned snails into snail shells. Put under the broiler until the butter has completely melted and is sizzling hot. Or dot the Butter for Snails on fish fillets 5 minutes before they finish broiling.

Shallot Butter

½ cup butter	2 Tbs. parsley, minced
3 Tbs. shallots, minced	

Cream the butter in a small bowl, and crush the minced shallots into the butter. Beat with the parsley into the butter, then chill.

Butter for Snails

½ cup butter
2 Tbs. shallots, minced
2 cloves garlic, minced
2 Tbs. parsley, minced
Salt and pepper to taste

Whip the butter until soft. Crush the shallots and garlic into the butter and beat together with the parsley; salt and pepper to taste.

Sorrel (*Rumex,* all species)

There are two types of sorrel used in cooking, an annual known as French sorrel (*Rumex scutatus*), and a perennial called garden sorrel (*Rumex acetosa*). The French type is smaller and has a stronger flavor. It is the type used to make sorrel soup, a famous delicacy, and the one whose leaves are preferred for salads. The flowers of French sorrel are often dried and used to make winter bouquets of flowers. Use the leaves with combinations of more bland salad greens. To serve French sorrel as a vegetable, cook the leaves in just a little water, stirring constantly, and remove from the heat as soon as they are limp. Drain well, dry over the heat, and add butter and salt to taste. Mince a few sorrel leaves into soups with a creamy base, and into omelets, as they finish cooking. Sorrel is used fresh, not dried, as flavoring.

Culture: Plant the seeds of either annual or perennial sorrel in rich, most soil in full sunlight. Sow in shallow drills, 1 inch deep, and cover with ½ inch fine soil. Tamp. Thin the seedlings to 8 inches when they reach 3 inches in height. The perennial sorrel plants are hardy to −20°, and will come back year after year. The annual sorrel will die at the end of the first season, and must be planted again the following year.

The recipe below is one of the best-known sorrel dishes, a gourmet specialty offered at good French restaurants.

Sorrel Soup

⅓ cup onion, peeled and minced
2 Tbs. butter
3 cups tightly packed sorrel leaves
½ tsp. salt
3 Tbs. all-purpose flour
5½ cups hot chicken broth
2 egg yolks
½ cup heavy cream
2 Tbs. soft butter
3 fresh sorrel leaves

1. In a large saucepan, simmer the onions in the butter until translucent. Stir in the sorrel leaves and the salt, cover, and simmer 5 minutes, or until the leaves are tender and completely wilted. Sprinkle the flour over the greens, and stir to mix. Stirring continually and very quickly, pour the hot broth over the greens. Stir while the greens simmer 5 minutes more. Put through a blender at slow speed, 1 cup at a time, to purée the sorrel. Return to low heat.
2. In a large cup, mix the yolks together, and stir into them a little of the hot soup. Return the contents of the cup to the saucepan, add the cream, and stir while it heats through. Do not allow the soup to boil. Beat in the butter, and serve at once. For a garnish, float a few fresh sorrel leaves on the soup.

Serves 4 to 6.

Southernwood (*Artemisia abrotanum*)

Southernwood is a fragrance that belongs in the same genus as tarragon, *Artemisia dracunculus,* and wormwood, *Artemisia absinthium.* The sagebrush of the Western plains is another of the Artemisias. Southernwood leaves have a delicate lemony scent and today are used primarily to scent linens and protect woolens from moths.

In the past, southernwood was an important medicinal herb rather than a fragrance herb. As a medicinal herb, it dates back beyond the Roman Empire. Balding is one of the ailments ancient herbalists thought it would cure — the herb was burned and the ashes mixed with oil and applied to the head. (Today it is said that young country boys still use an ointment of southernwood ashes for growing beards.) Southernwood was once

Southernwood

Southernwood and Roses Moth Repellent

2 cups dried laven-
der buds
1 cup dried rose
leaves

1 cup dried south-
ernwood
2 drops of oil of
roses

Crush all the ingredients together, cover, and cure in a small crock for 4 weeks. Shake up the contents every day or two. Divide among small muslin bags, tie the bags, and place them among the woolens.

also considered a heady ingredient for love potions. *Banckes's* (sic) *Herbal* says, "The virtue of this herb is thus, that if they break the seed and drink it with water, it healest men that have been bitten by any venimous beasts." Southernwood was often used to create little clipped hedges of gray foliage for the knot gardens and parterres that developed about the time of Elizabeth I.

Culture: Southernwood is a perennial, hardy to about −10°. It will grow to between 3 and 5 feet tall if unclipped, and prefers a dry, sandy soil and lots of sun. Some of the varieties offered by seedsmen have been bred to intensify the silvery effect of the foliage, and these are exceptionally attractive in the flowering border, and herb garden, or grown in containers in groups of 6 or more. Southernwood does well as a houseplant if constantly clipped back. Prune southernwood early in its life and often to increase low branching. Indoors, grow it under lights or on your sunniest windowsill.

This recipe combining southernwood and roses is used as a moth repellent.

Sweet Woodruff (*Asperula odorata*)

Sweet woodruff flowers are used in flavoring May wine, and are also steeped in boiling water to make an herbal tea. Woodruff carries the wonderful fragrance of newly mown hay and was a favorite strewing herb in both England and colonial America. Today it is used perhaps most often to scent sachets and bags for linens and closets, and as a fragrant ground cover.

Woodruff's history as an herb goes back many centuries. It was one of the dried herbs hung in room corners to sweeten the air, and along with sprays of lavender buds, it was made into garlands and placed in churches in colonial America and in fourteenth century England. Since it grows close to the ground, it has been used as a scented ground cover since herb gardens first began. Medicinally, the leaves were applied to small cuts to stop bleeding. "It is good for healing all sicknesses that come from heat," according to *Hortus Sanitatis*, an ancient herbal.

Culture: A perennial, hardy to about −20°, woodruff is best grown from root divisions planted in mid-spring. Woodruff spreads by underground roots and will multiply rapidly if the soil conditions are right. Plant in slight shade, in rich, moist soil. Woodruff needs to freeze in winter, and so doesn't do well as a houseplant. It is about 8 inches high at maturity.

The recipe below is one typical of those used to make homemade May wine.

Sweet Woodruff

May Wine Punch

12 tips of fresh
  woodruff, slightly
  crushed
1½ cups superfine
  sugar

1 bottle Moselle or
  dry white wine
1 bottle champagne
12 fresh, ripe
  strawberries

1. In a large bowl, combine woodruff, sugar, and 1 bottle of Moselle or dry white wine. Cover, and steep for 30 minutes.
2. Remove the cover, stir the mixture, remove the woodruff, and pour the wine over ice in a punch bowl. Add the remaining ingredients, stir, and serve as soon as thoroughly chilled.
Serves 16 to 20.

Tansy (*Tanacetum vulgare*)

A flavoring and medicinal herb in ages past, tansy today is grown mainly for use in tussie-mussies and dried bouquets. Tansy is also used as a moth repellent, and is believed by many gardeners to repel insects.

In the Middle Ages it was recommended as a cure for all sorts of ailments associated with colic, and with ills such as gout which then were related to overeating. It was brewed to make teas as a preventive against "summer complaints." The leaves were applied to ease the effects of sunburn and were believed to remove freckles and other skin blemishes. In colonial America, the herb had many medicinal uses, and some culinary uses, but because of the somewhat toxic natures of the leaves, it was used sparingly and eventually fell out of favor.

Culture: Tansy is often found growing wild by roadsides and in fields: It is a perennial herb brought here by European colonials, and escaped from early gardens. A strongly scented plant that grows rapidly to 2 or 3 feet, tansy bears bright yellow button-like flowers in flat clusters. Plant seeds, or root divisions, in any well-worked soil in a sunny

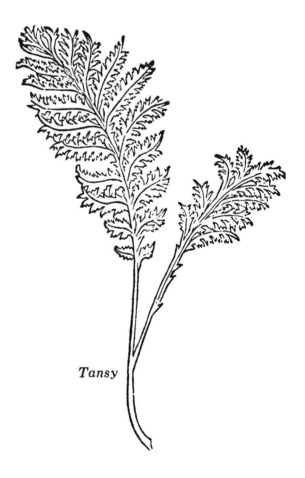

Tansy

exposure. The bright green leaves are finely cut as ferns, and look pretty in the flower border or in groups in containers on the terrace. A variety, *Tanacetum vulgare crispum,* is the best choice if tansy is to be grown as an ornamental.

A recipe using tansy for fragrance in a moth bag combines it with southernwood.

Tansy Moth Bags

3 cups dried southernwood	2 cups dried tansy leaves
2 cups dried thyme	⅓ cup ground cloves

Crush all the ingredients together in a bowl, and divide among small muslin bags. Tie the bags firmly, and place among woolens.

Tarragon
(*Artemisia dracunculus*)

Tarragon is one of the best of the flavoring herbs. Stuff poultry with sprigs of fresh tarragon before cooking, and remove the herbs before serving. Dress fish to be baked with fresh tarragon, and drizzle with melted butter. Use 1 teaspoon fresh tarragon, minced, in cream sauces, in tartar sauce, with seafood and egg salads, and in marinades for shishkebabs. Tarragon vinegar is a specialty you can make yourself, and one that does wonders for any salad. The dried herb is excellent in any veal or lamb dish, in cooked casseroles, and is one of the important ingredients in Green Goddess dressing and Sauce Béarnaise. Tarragon has a strong fragrance and is often used in the making of potpourris.

A native of Siberia, tarragon seems to have appeared in Europe in about the thirteenth century. Its name is derived from the Greek word for dragon, a name that may relate to the serpentine formation of tarragon roots. In French, tarragon is *estragon,* and in Spanish *taragona.* It doesn't appear often in the old herbals, but Ibn Baithar, a Spaniard of the thirteenth century, refers to it as good

Tarragon

cooked with vegetables, and says the juice is used to flavor drinks, sweeten the breath, disguise bitter medicine, and taken as an aid to sleep.

Culture: Tarragon is a perennial, hardy to about −20°, and about 20 inches tall. It is best grown from root divisions, or rooted cuttings. The plants grown in this country apparently don't set seed. When buying tarragon plants, crush the leaves to make sure that they are strongly aromatic: Some plants are less desirable than others. Once you have tarragon, you can multiply your holdings by taking tip cuttings in August. Set plants out in mid-spring, in moderately rich soil that is well drained. Place tarragon in sunlight, or in semi-sun. In fall, you can bring the plant indoors, and keep it growing for some time in a sunny window sill. If it begins to fail, try it in the refrigerator for a month or so, and it may come back.

Tarragon vinegar can be made following the recipe below. The marinade that follows is wonderful with leftover vegetables. Clam sauce is one of the great Italian dishes flavored with tarragon.

Tarragon Vinegar

1 cup tightly packed tip sprigs of fresh tarragon	1 quart white wine vinegar
	1 long sprig fresh tarragon

1. Bruise the leaves in the bottom of a bowl, and press them into a 1-quart canning jar. Bring the vinegar to boiling point, but do not boil, and pour at once over the herbs, leaving 2 inches of headroom. Cap the jar tightly. Marinate the contents in a warm room for 10 days, shaking the jar often. Taste the vinegar. If it is not strong enough in flavor, strain out the herbs, crush a fresh cupful, pour the vinegar over it, and marinate 10 days more.
2. Strain the vinegar through a clean piece of cheesecloth. Scald a long, fresh sprig of tarragon leaves for 15 seconds in boiling water, press into a vinegar bottle, pour the tarragon vinegar over it. Cap tightly.

Marinade with Tarragon for Vegetables

½ cup olive oil	1 clove garlic, peeled and minced
3 Tbs. strained lemon juice	
3 Tbs. cider vinegar	2 Tbs. minced, fresh tarragon or 1 Tbs. dried
⅛ tsp. pepper	
1 tsp. salt	

Combine all the ingredients and beat for 2 minutes, or process in a blender for 1 minute at low speed. Pour over warm vegetables and allow to marinate for several hours before serving.

Makes ¾ cup.

Francesca Bosetti Morris's Linguini with White Clam Sauce

¼ cup olive oil	2 6½ oz. cans of minced clams, or 2 cups fresh minced clams
2 cloves garlic, peeled and crushed	
Liquor from clams	¼ cup parsley, chopped
½ cup dry white wine	Salt and pepper to taste
2 Tbs. fresh tarragon, or 1 Tbs. dried	4 portions cooked linguini

1. In a medium saucepan, heat the oil and brown the garlic. Add the liquor from the clams, and the wine. When these are hot, add the tarragon. Cover, simmer about 3 minutes to bring out the tarragon flavor. Add the clams and parsley. Cook just long enough to heat the clams through. Add salt and pepper to taste.
2. Combine hot linguini, cooked *al dente* (just barely), with the hot sauce, and serve at once.

Serves 4 portions.

Thyme (*Thymus,* all species)

The low growth and intense scent of thyme makes it one of the herbs preferred for ground covers, as well as for flavoring and for use in dry perfumes. As a scent herb, it is used in tussie-mussies, in sachets, as a moth repellent, in rubbing vinegars, to make bath lotions, bags for herbal baths, and all manner of fragrant things. As a culinary herb, it is used in gumbos, in *bouillabaisse,* in fish and shellfish chowders, in onion dishes, with boiled carrots, beets, in stuffings for fowl and in sauces and butters to go with almost everything. Parisians sprinkle dried thyme on steaks before broiling, and herb fans brew it into a tea.

The scent of thyme was a favorite personal fragrance among Greeks, for it was a symbol of elegance. Among the Romans, thyme was considered medicine potent against depression. In Elizabeth I's day, it was a favorite of the herb garden for flavor, for scent, and for its magical properties. A recipe dated 1600, to "Enable One To See The Fairies," included thyme. In the language of the plants, it is associated with happiness and with courage.

Culture: Thymus serpyllum, Mother-of-Thyme, has white, rose or crimson flowers, and is grown all over the country as a ground cover. It reaches only a few inches in height. Lemon thyme, which has lemon-scented foliage, is a variety of Mother-of-Thyme. *Thymus vulgaris* is considered the best species to grow for flavoring. It gets to be 6 to 10 inches tall. Both are perennials, and both can be used for flavoring. *Thymus vulgaris*

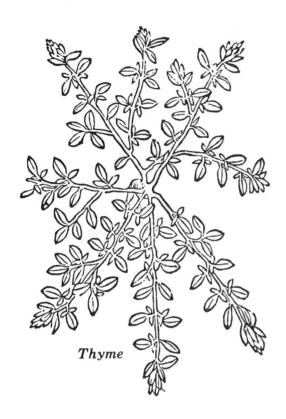

Thyme

1 sprig fresh pars-
ley, or 1 tsp.
dried
6 peppercorns
1 small carrot

1 medium onion,
stuck with 5
whole cloves
1 Tbs. salt

Tie all the ingredients into a cheesecloth bag, and add to water for cooking fish, lobster, crabs, chicken, veal. This quantity flavors 2 quarts of cooking water.

Oil and Vinegar Dressing

6 Tbs. olive oil, or
vegetable oil
1½ Tbs. vinegar
⅛ tsp. dry mustard
¼ tsp. granulated
sugar

1 tsp. salt
⅛ tsp. pepper
2 tsp. minced fresh
thyme, or 1 tsp.
dried

Process all ingredients in a blender set at low for 1 minute.
Makes ¼ cup.

Violet (*Viola,* all species)

Violets aren't thought of as herbs for cooking, but in point of fact, the violet flowers are edible, and were used in cuisine as well as for fragrance and medicinal purposes in earlier centuries. Candied violets are among the most charming of garnishes for cakes and desserts: Combined with candied mint leaves, they make delightful bonbons for gift giving. The flowers of truly fragrant species, dried and mixed in with potpourris, add a color note as well as a hint of violet perfume.

Violet blossoms were used as soup herbs, sauce herbs, and salad herbs long ago, and violet leaves went into omelets. Violet fritters were a delicacy, and violets garnished a type of custard called *mon ami,* "my friend." In the language of the plants, violets have been symbols of sweetness and humility and faithfulness since the days of ancient Greece. It is a flower associated with romance. Marie Antoinette loved the scent, and it was one of the preferred fragrances of Josephine, the lovely Creole Napoleon married. Violets are mentioned in the tussie-mussie Ophelia prepared for Hamlet. In *Banckes's* (sic) *Herbal,* violets were recommended in a mixture with

makes a good edging plant, and one to grow over rocks. Select started plants, as seed packets don't always produce the best thymes, if you plan to grow a few specimens as potted plants or in the indoor garden. For thyme to be used as ground cover, sow seeds, or take cuttings or make root divisions of a friend's thyme plants. Germination of seeds takes 15 to 21 days outdoors, and about 10 days indoors. Plant thyme in mid-spring in sandy soil that is dryish. Full sunlight is necessary for thyme to flourish. Keep container and pot plants clipped to encourage bushiness.

Thyme as a flavoring for boiled dishes, stocks, and soups and stews is often combined with the ingredients below. The Oil and Vinegar Dressing recipe given here, without thyme, is a classic French dressing you can use as a base for any herb-flavored salad.

Herbs for a Court Bouillon

1 bay leaf
1 tsp. dried thyme

2 branches celery
with leaves

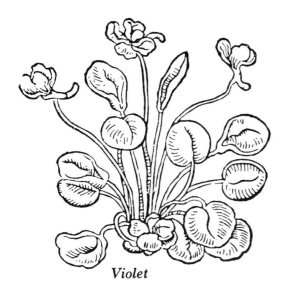

Violet

Candied Violets

2 oz. gum arabic	1 Tbs. white corn
1 cup water	syrup
24 fresh violet	Red and blue food
blossoms	coloring
2 cups sugar	¼ cup superfine
½ cup water	sugar

1. In the top of the double boiler over boiling water, stir the gum arabic with 1 cup of water until dissolved. Cool. With a fork, dip the violets into the mixture, coating all surfaces. Dry on waxed paper 2 hours.
2. In a small saucepan, bring 2 cups of sugar, the ½ cup water, and the corn syrup to a boil, and cook — but don't stir — until it reaches 234° on the candy thermometer. Stir in enough drops of red and blue food coloring to produce a color similar to that of your violets. Allow the syrup to cool to lukewarm.
3. Color the remaining sugar with red and blue to create violet. Allow the sugar to dry on waxed papers: press out any lumps.
4. Dip each blossom in the cooled syrup, drain, place head down in the colored sugar. Dust the blossoms with colored sugar. Let dry overnight, or until hardened, then store in air-tight, moisture-free container. Use as a garnish on desserts.

pounded poppy seeds as a cure for fevers, for sore eyes, and falling fits and drunkenness.

Culture: The violet grown for fragrance is *Viola odorata,* the sweet violet, a perennial 8 to 12 inches tall, hardy to about −20°. Select the most fragrant variety available, and start seeds indoors, or buy root divisions and plant these in early spring or mid-fall. I find violets flower heavily in less-rich soil. They need some shelter from midday summer sun, should never go dry, and in really hot regions, should be planted in semi-shade. Sweet violets spread by means of a root system that looks like a small tuber, and they self-sow seeds. The name varieties 'Royal Robe' and 'White Czar' have wonderfully bright leaves that look well in flower borders as edgings, even when the plants are out of bloom. (They are perennials: Started from seed they won't blossom until the second season.) African violets aren't true violets, but the flowers look remarkably like violets. They can be candied, too. African violets are the type to grow indoors, as real violets don't stand up to house culture. Flowers of single-flowered 'Blue Boy' varieties are best for candying.

One way in which violet blossoms are candied appears below.

Wormwood (*Artemisia,* all species)

Wormwood is the name given to several members of the Artemisia genus which have been used medicinally, and for flavor and fragrance, in the past. The best-known use of *Artemisia absinthium* — common wormwood — is as the flavoring in absynthe, an alcoholic beverage outlawed in its homeland, France. In absynthe, apparently the herb had a toxic effect that caused hallucinations and could lead to madness. The fine leaves of this member of the wormwood group have a bitter taste, and are today used only spar-

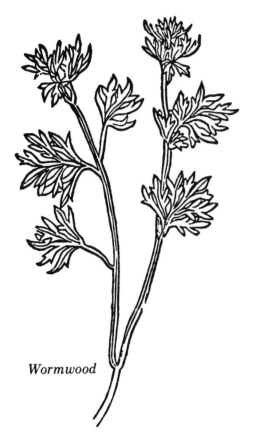

Wormwood

putteth away all manner of impediments of the sight. It is good to comfort the heart."

Culture: Wormwood, like the other artemisias, has attractive pale silver foliage, and is often used in the herb garden and in the flowering border as a foliage accent. Two to 4 feet tall, it blends especially beautifully with gardens where blue or pink are the colors predominating. Wormwood is a perennial, hardy to about −20°. It will grow anywhere, but preferably in full sun, in dry soil that isn't too fertile; however, it will survive in a shady location, though it may not thrive there. *Artemisia absinthium* grows to be between 2 and 4 feet tall. Roman wormwood and old woman, or dusty miller, *(Artemisia stelleriana),* and *Artemisia schmidtiana Nana,* 'Silver Mound' variety, are smaller plants with good gray color. Grow wormwood as a container plant, or indoors — keep potted artemisias pruned, as they tend to get straggly.

For use as a moth preventive, wormwood is used here with sharp-scented mint, tansy, and thyme.

Wormwood Moth Bags

1 cup dried wormwood	1 cup dried tansy
1 cup dried spearmint	1 cup dried thyme
	4 cinnamon sticks

In a bowl, combine all the ingredients, then crush them together. Divide the mixture among small muslin bags, tie securely, and place with the woolens.

ingly to flavor poultry, to scent sachets, and to keep moths away.

Wormwood was one of the herbs used in vinegars to keep away the plague, and it was thought that to carry a sprig of it prevented fatigue on long voyages. The juice of wormwood "mingled with sweet milk is good for worms" according to *Banckes's* (sic) *Herbal,* and when "pounded with the gall of a bull it

Appendix

Sources, Organizations

A list of seedsmen who sell herbs by mail follows. It does not pretend to include all those selling herbs, but only companies that have for some time been established as mail order suppliers. When ordering herbs for your garden, specify the type you want — don't accept just any, or just what the seedsman you have elected proposes, or mails back.

Ashby's Garden Centre & Nursery, Cameron, Ontario, Canada.

Barr, Clause, Prairie Gem Ranch, Smithwick, S. D. 57782

Black Forest Botanicals, Route 1, Box 34, Yuba, Wisc. 54672

Bluemont Nurseries, P.O. Box 219, Monkton, Md. 21111

Borchelt Herb Gardens, East Falmouth, Mass. 02536

Burpee, W. Atlee, Co., 300 Park Ave., Warminster, Pa. 18974

Cakumet Herb Company, P.O. Box 248, South Holland, Ill. 60473

Cape Code Nurseries, P.O. Drawer B., Falmouth, Mass. 02541

Caprilands Herb Farm, Coventry, Conn. 06238

Carobil Farm, Church Road, Brunswick, Me. 04011

Carroll Gardens, Westminster, Md. 21157

Cedarbrook Herb Farm, Sequim, Wash. 98382

Central Nursery Company, 2657 Johnson Ave., San Luis Obispo, Calif. 93401

Chientan & Co., 1001 S. Alvarado St., Los Angeles, Calif. 90006

Comstock, Ferre & Co., Wethersfield, Conn. 06109

Cottage Herb Farm Shop, 311 State St., Albany, N.Y. 12210

Edmund's Native Plant Nursery, 2190 Oak Grove Rd. Walnut Creek, Calif. 94589

Exeter Wild Flower Gardens, Exeter, N.H. 03883

Greene Herb Gardens, Greene, R.I. 02898

Gurney Seed Co., Yankton, S.D. 59078

Harris, Joseph, Co., Moreton Farm, Rochester, N.Y. 14624

Hart Seed Co., Wethersfield, Conn. 06109

Hemlock Hill Herb Farm, Litchfield, Conn. 06759

The Herb Farm, Barnard Rd., Granville, Mass. 01034

The Herb House, P.O. Box 308, Beaumont, Calif. 92223

The Herb Store, Sherman Oaks, Calif. 91403

Herbs Alive and Potted, 347 E. 55th St., New York, N.Y. 10022

Hilltop Herb Farm, P.O. Box 866, Cleveland, Tex. 77327

House of Herbs, 459 Eighteenth Ave., Newark, N.J. 07108

Hudson, J.L., P.O. Box 1058, Redwood City, Calif. 04064

Jamieson Valley Gardens, Route 3, Spokane, Wash. 99203

Leodar Nurseries, 7206 Belvedere Road, West Palm Beach, Fla. 33406

Leslie's Wildflower Nursery, 30 Summer St., Methuen, Mass. 01884

Logee's Greenhouses, 55 North St., Danielson, Conn. 06239

Lounsberry Gardens, Oakford, Ill. 62673

Mail Box Seeds, 2042 Encinal Ave., Alameda, Calif. 94501

Merry Gardens, Camden, Me. 04843

Michael's Garden Gate, Mt. Kisco, N.Y. 10549

Mincemoyer Nursery, Box 482, Jackson, N.J. 08527

Murchie's, 1008 Robson St., Vancouver 105, B.C., Canada

Nichols Garden Nursery, 1190 N. Pacific Highway, Albany, Ore. 97321

Oakhurst Gardens, Arcadia, Calif. 91006

Orchid Gardens, Box 224, Grand Rapids, Mich. 55744

Park, George W., Seed Co., Greenwood, S.C. 29646

Payne, Theodore, Foundation, 10459 Tux-

ford St., Sun Valley, Calif. 91352

Penn Herb Co., 603 N. Second St., Philadelphia, Pa. 19123

Putney Nursery, Putney, Vt. 05346

Richter, Otto, & Sons, Ltd., Locust Hill, Ontario, Canada

Robin, Clude, P.O. Box 2091, Castro, Calif. 94546

Rocky Hollow Herb Farm, Sussex, N.J. 07461

The Rosemary House, Mechanicsburg, Pa. 17055

Roth, H. & Son, 1577 First Ave., New York, N.Y. 10028

Shop in the Sierra, P.O. Box 1, Midpines, Calif. 95345

Shuttle Hill Herb Shop, Delmar, N.Y. 12054

Sunnybrook Herb Farm Nursery, Mayfield Rd., Chesterfield, Ohio 44026

Taylor's Garden, 2649 Stingle Ave., Rosemead, Calif. 91770

The Tool Shed, North Salem, N.Y. 12865

Wayside Gardens, Mentor, Ohio 44060

White Flower Farm, Litchfield, Conn. 06759

Index